TIME FOR KIDS

That's Incredible!

THE WORLD'S MOST UNBELIEVABLE FACTS & RECORDS

20

TIME FOR KIDS That's Incredible!

TIME FOR KIDS
Managing Editor, TIME FOR KIDS: Nellie Gonzalez Cutler
Editor, Time Learning Ventures: Jonathan Rosenbloom

Created by: R studio T Design, New York City
Art Direction & Design: Raúl Rodriguez and Rebecca Tachna
Writer: Curtis Slepian
Photo Researchers: Miriam Budnick, Elizabeth Vezzulla
Copyeditor: Joe Bomba
Fact-Checkers: Mary Anne Greczyn, Danny Messing, Audrey Whitley
Acknowledgements: Diane, Georgina, and Terri at The Bone Room, Betsy Gabler at Alchemy, Prem Kalliat, New York Road Runners, Amanda Perin, Sophie Tachna, John Whitley

TIME HOME ENTERTAINMENT
Publisher: Richard Fraiman
General Manager: Steven Sandonato
Executive Director, Marketing Services: Carol Pittard
Executive Director, Retail & Special Sales: Tom Mifsud
Executive Director, New Product Development: Peter Harper
Director, Bookazine Development & Marketing: Laura Adam
Publishing Director, Brand Marketing: Joy Butts
Assistant General Counsel: Helen Wan
Design & Prepress Manager: Anne-Michelle Gallero
Book Production Manager: Susan Chodakiewicz
Associate Marketing Manager: Jonathan White
Associate Prepress Manager: Alex Voznesenskiy

Special Thanks to: Christine Austin, Jeremy Biloon, Alex Borinstein, Glenn Buonocore, Malati Chavali, Jim Childs, Rose Cirrincione, Jacqueline Fitzgerald, Christine Font, Lauren Hall, Carrie Hertan, Suzanne Janso, Raphael Joa, Jeffrey Kaji, Mona Li, Robert Marasco, Kimberly Marshall, Amy Migliaccio, Nina Mistry, Richard Prue, Dave Rozzelle, Myles Ringel, Ilene Schreider, Sasha Shapiro, Soren Shapiro, Adriana Tierno, Time Imaging, Vanessa Wu

For information on TIME For Kids magazine for the classroom or home, go to WWW.TFKCLASSROOM.COM or call 1-800-777-8600.

For subscriptions to Sports Illustrated Kids, go to www.sikids.com or call 1-800-889-6007.

Published by TIME For Kids Books
Time Inc.
1271 Avenue of the Americas
New York, New York 10020

ISBN 10: 1-60320-199-8
ISBN 13: 978-1-60320-199-5
Library of Congress No.: 2011929052

We welcome your comments and suggestions about TIME For Kids Books. Please write to us at:
TIME For Kids Books
Attention: Book Editors
PO Box 11016
Des Moines, IA 50336-1016

If you would like to order any of our hardcover Collector's Edition books, please call us at 1-800-327-6388. (Monday through Friday, 7:00 a.m.– 8:00 p.m. or Saturday, 7:00 a.m.– 6:00 p.m. Central Time).

1 TLF 11

Contents

It's an Incredible World! ---------- 6

1 Incredible Size ---------- 8
Super-Size Squid ---------- 10
Prehistoric Predators ---------- 12
Ship Shapes ---------- 14
Big Movers and Shakers ---------- 16
Big, Big Bubbles ---------- 18
Living Large ---------- 20
Give Him a Big Hand ---------- 22
Artists Think Big–and Small ---------- 24
The Incredible Shrinking White House ---------- 26
Big City, Small Town ---------- 28
Good Things Come in Small Packages ---------- 30

2 Incredible Animals and Plants ---------- 32
Introducing…New Animals ---------- 34
Animal Suckers ---------- 36
Funny Faces ---------- 38
Old Timers ---------- 40
A Dragon's Tale ---------- 42
Great Performances ---------- 44
Cool Cats ---------- 46
Disappearing Acts ---------- 48
Mixed-Up Animals ---------- 50
Creating a Stink ---------- 52
Animal Smarts ---------- 54
Top Pops ---------- 56
Road Trips ---------- 58
Amazing Frogs ---------- 60

3 Incredible Sports ---------- 62
All-Time Record Breakers ---------- 64
Masked Marvels ---------- 66
Strange Sports ---------- 68
Off to the Races ---------- 70
Sports Bloopers… ---------- 72
…and Blunders ---------- 74
Pros and Pets ---------- 76
Extreme Snowmobiling ---------- 78

37

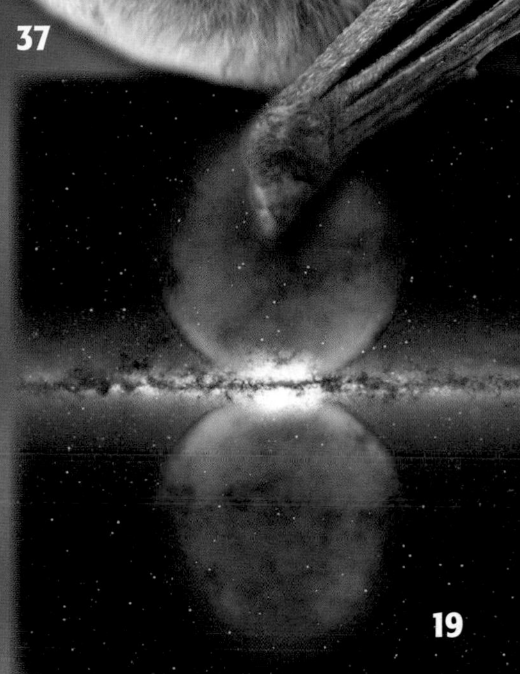

19

48

61

75

93

4 Incredible Food ---------- 80
Chocolate Dreams ---------- 82
It Looks Good Enough to Eat ---------- 84

5 Incredible Arts ---------- 86
Sand-Sational Sculptures ---------- 88
Feats of Clay ---------- 90
Face It! ---------- 92

6 Incredible Earth ---------- 94
Killer Waves ---------- 96
Extreme Geography ---------- 98
The World at Night ---------- 100
Gem-Dandy! ---------- 102
Peak Experiences ---------- 104
Nature Rocks! ---------- 106
Underground Wonderlands ---------- 108

7 Incredible Space ---------- 110
Cosmic Collisions ---------- 112
The Solar System's Wonders ---------- 114
Making a Huge Impact ---------- 116
Here Comes the Sun ---------- 118
Galactic Garbage ---------- 120

8 Incredible Collections ---------- 122
Collector's Items ---------- 124
Curious Collections ---------- 126
Odd Museums ---------- 128

9 Incredible Jobs ---------- 130
They Wow the World ---------- 132
Thrilling Careers ---------- 134

10 Incredible Technology ---------- 136
Fun and Games ---------- 138
Great Inventions ---------- 140
Ultimate Bicycles ---------- 142
Just Plane Amazing ---------- 144
Which One Is Real? ---------- 146
Green Giants ---------- 148
Bring on the Bots ---------- 150

106

128

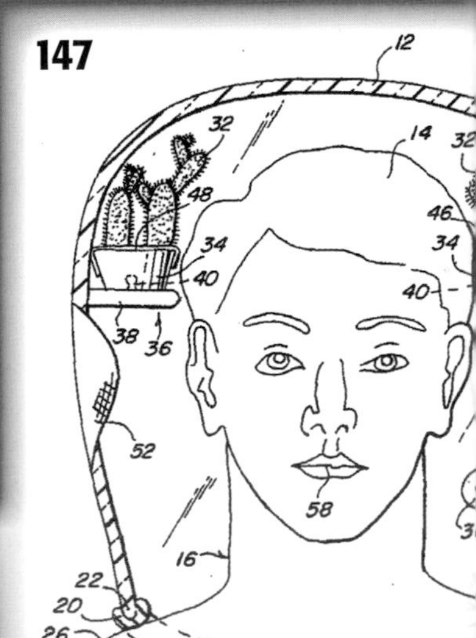

147

115

11 **Incredible Human Body** ---------- 152
An Inside Look ---------- 154
Technology for Life ---------- 156
Who Needs These Body Parts? ---------- 158
The Amazing Human Body Quiz ---------- 160

12 **Incredible Mysteries** ---------- 162
The Hoax Hall of Fame ---------- 164
Tales of the Unknown ---------- 166
Do Monsters Exist? ---------- 168

13 **Incredible Constructions** ---------- 170
These Walls Are Alive! ---------- 172
Those Wild and Crazy Buildings ---------- 174
Bodacious Bridges ---------- 176
A-maze-ing Mazes ---------- 178

14 **Incredible Micro Worlds** ---------- 180
Nano Wonders ---------- 182
Buggin' Out ---------- 184

15 **Incredible Kids** ---------- 186
Kids Conquer the World ---------- 188
Kids Make a Big Difference ---------- 190

16 **Incredibly Weird But True** ---------- 192
Now That's Weird! ---------- 194
Now That's Weirder! ---------- 196

Where in the World? ---------- 198

Index ---------- 200
Credits ---------- 206
R U in the Hunt? ---------- 208

164

188

153

196

It's an Incredible World!

This book will take you on a tour of the most incredible things the universe has to offer, from galaxies that collide to the tiniest frog on Earth, from ships as tall as skyscrapers to a portrait made of breakfast cereal. In these pages, you'll discover incredible facts, surprising information, and loads of eye-popping photos. When you read it, you'll definitely be saying, "Now that's incredible!"

Where can you find sand sculptures based on hit movies? Travel to Incredible Arts.

Where can you find a rock 'n roll museum? Turn to Incredible Constructions.

Who sealed himself inside a block of ice for 63 hours? Go to Incredible Jobs.

How many people live in the smallest city in the world? Head over to Incredible Size.

Where is the world's longest mountain range? Dive into Incredible Earth.

Incredible!

You'll find mind-boggling facts in every chapter. They'll make you shake your head in wonder.

Actual Size

0 Inch 1

The ruler signals that the object you're seeing on the page is actual size.

For the Record

This box features cool stats and information.

Where is the tallest mountain in the solar system? The answer is in Incredible Space.

BTW

On many pages you'll see BTW (By The Way) boxes, where you'll discover surprising facts or background on the subject.

What snowboarder blundered in the 2006 Winter Olympics? Slide over to Incredible Sports.

What world landmark has been copied in chocolate? Look to Incredible Foods.

Where does the Abominable Snowman supposedly live? Learn in Incredible Mysteries.

What is the biggest frog in the world? Hop over to Incredible Animals.

Who sailed around the world at age 16? Cruise on over to Incredible Kids.

Blast from the Past

Your place to find interesting historical facts about what you're reading.

Chapter 1 Incredible Size

Big stuff gets our attention: big buildings, big airplanes, big screens, big meals, big athletes. Small, on the other hand, doesn't seem to be such a big deal. That's why we have expressions like "small potatoes" and "small talk." But if you look closely, you'll see that a small wonder can be as cool as a big deal. No matter how you measure it, the worlds of the large and the little are both incredible.

In This Chapter

- Prehistoric Predators in All Sizes
- Teeny Houses
- The Biggest Squid Ever
- The White House in Miniature

And Much More!

Actual Size

0 Inch 1

BTW

It's one of the world's biggest bugs. Find out the name of this incredible insect on page 20.

For the Record

Tenney, Minnesota, is the least populous city in the U.S. According to the 2000 Census, it had a population of six. The population actually went down from six to two shortly after the 2000 Census was taken.

Hope
I don't get a
flat tire!

Incredible!

A scale model of the White House includes a tiny rug that's an exact copy of one in the First Family's home. Only this rug is much smaller: 22 inches by 32 inches. With 900 stitches in every square inch, it took 3½ years to complete.

BTW

The **LeTourneau** (leh-tor-*noh*) is a front end loader that's the size of a small apartment, with wheels almost twice the height of a person. It can lift 160,000 pounds of dirt, snow, rocks, logs, or whatever else needs to be loaded into a dump truck.

Super-Size Squid

The giant squid is camera shy. Until recently, no one had ever seen this creature alive. Scientists had been able to study only a few body parts washed up on shore, hauled in by fishers, or found in the stomach of a whale. But in 2006, Japanese scientists were able to catch a giant squid. The squid was about 24 feet long. Unfortunately, it died soon after the scientists brought it to the surface.

For the Record

Giant squids are the largest invertebrates in the world. (Invertebrates are animals without backbones.) They average about 33 feet in length and weigh about 440 pounds. One was 59 feet long and weighed nearly 2,000 pounds.

A giant squid has a sharp, beak-like mouth. It eats fish, shrimp, other squid, and sometimes, even whale!

Like other squids, the giant version has eight arms, plus two longer tentacles that are used to bring food to the mouth. The arms and tentacles are lined with suckers—cups that can grab and hold onto prey.

The giant squid's eyes are about 10 inches across, making them the biggest peepers in the animal kingdom. Their eyes are larger than a human head. Large eyes allow the giant squid to see in the dim light of the ocean depths.

Blast from the Past

A giant squid once attacked a submarine—in a science-fiction novel, that is. *Twenty Thousand Leagues Under the Sea* was written by Jules Verne in 1869. In one scene in the novel, a submarine named the *Nautilus* runs into a giant squid. The sea monster attacks sailors and the sub, but it is fought off by the crewmembers and their captain, Nemo.

Incredible!

The colossal squid might be larger than the giant squid. Only a few have ever been found, but scientists estimate it can grow as long as 46 feet, with a wider, heavier body than the giant squid.

Prehistoric Predators

Dinosaurs lived from about 228 million years ago to 65 million years ago. During some of that time, dinosaurs shared the planet with mammals and other reptiles. Both dinosaurs and non-dinosaurs came in sizes both extra **large** and extra small.

X, the Unknown Creature

T. rex was the baddest dude among dinosaurs. But scientists have found the fossil of a reptile that makes *Tyrannosaurus rex* look like a wimp. **Predator X** was a pliosaur (*ply*-uh-sore), a reptile that ruled the seas more than 147 million years ago. It was 50 feet long and had 12-inch-long teeth. Its 10-foot-long head was twice as big as a T. rex skull. Predator X was also stronger and heavier than T. rex. At 45 tons, it outweighed the king of dinos by six or seven tons.

X is 12 times longer than I am tall!

Incredible!

During the age of dinosaurs, some mammals weren't afraid of dinos. Scientists recently discovered the fossil of an opposum-size mammal. It had in its stomach the remains of a baby dinosaur called a **psittacosaur**. It's the first evidence that mammals fed on small dinos.

Mini T. Rex

Tyrannosaurus rex was a ferocious, meat-eating dinosaur with a big head, powerful legs, tiny arms, and massive body. Imagine those traits on a beast 100 times lighter. That is a **raptorex**, a newly discovered species of tyrannosaur that was about eight feet long and weighed about 175 pounds. The dino lived about 125 million years ago, tens of millions of years earlier than its bigger cousin. Although the raptorex was smaller in size, it was just as fierce as its mighty cousin.

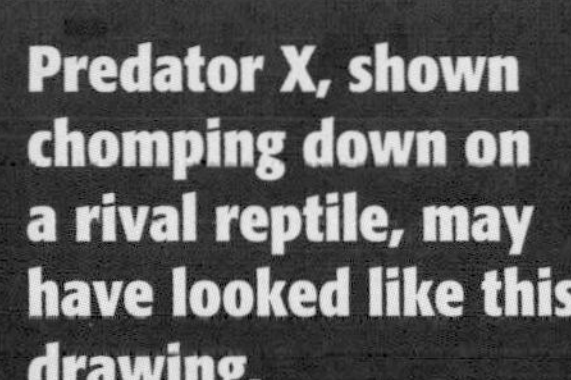

Predator X, shown chomping down on a rival reptile, may have looked like this drawing.

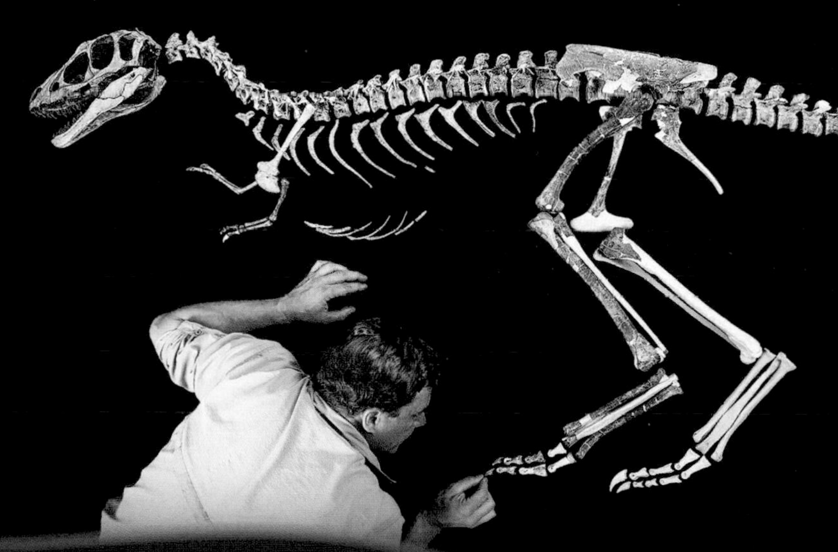

Biggest Ancient Animals

	LENGTH	WEIGHT (POUNDS)
1. Biggest snake: *Titanoboa cerrejonensis*	42 ft	2,500
2. Biggest rodent: *Josephoartigasia monesi*	10 ft	2,200
3. Biggest frog: *Beelzebufo*	16 in	10
4. Biggest Shark: *Carcharodon megalodon*	50 ft	150,000
5. Biggest penguin: *Inkayaku paracasensis*	5 ft	120

Source NATGEO News Watch

Ship Shapes

People have been building boats for at least 8,000 years. The first boats were called dugouts, made from hollowed-out trees. Later, they were built from wood planks. In the 1900s, when metal replaced wood, boats became larger and larger. Today, super-size vessels sail the seas—some as long as the tallest skyscrapers are high.

Amazing Aircraft Carrier

The **USS *Enterprise*** is the world's first nuclear-powered aircraft carrier. It is also one of the world's longest naval vessels. At a length of 1,123 feet and as high as a 40-story building, the ship was built from 120 million pounds of steel. *Enterprise* is also the fastest aircraft carrier, with a top speed of 40 miles per hour. Its home port is the naval station at Norfolk, Virginia. About 5,000 sailors keep *Enterprise* shipshape.

1,123 feet long

ALLURE OF THE SEAS
1,187 feet long
787 feet long
"All the News That's Fit to Print."
The New York Times.
NEW YORK, SATURDAY, MAY 8, 1915.—TWENTY-FOUR PAGES.
ONE CENT
LUSITANIA SUNK BY A SUBMARINE, PROBABLY 1,000 DEAD;
TWICE TORPEDOED OFF IRISH COAST; SINKS IN 15 MINUTES;
AMERICANS ABOARD INCLUDED VANDERBILT AND FROHMAN;
WASHINGTON BELIEVES THAT A GRAVE CRISIS IS AT HAND
Washington Deeply Stirred by Disaster and Fears a Crisis.
Loss of the Lusitania Fills London

Colossal Cruiser

The *Allure of the Seas* is the largest passenger ship in the world. At 1,187 feet long and 236 feet wide, it is reportedly two inches longer than its sister ship, *Oasis of the Seas*. As long as four football fields, the *Allure* has 16 passenger decks, a tree-lined park, an ice skating rink, and a 3-D movie theater. It can carry more than 6,300 passengers and has a crew of 2,384.

Blast from the Past

The *Lusitania* was the largest passenger ship in the world when it first set sail in 1906. In 1915, the British ship was sunk by a German submarine. Among the 1,195 who died were 128 U.S. citizens. Americans were angry, and the sinking became one of the reasons that the U.S. entered World War I in 1917.

Big Movers and Shakers

Big construction projects need huge vehicles to dig up dirt and haul heavy objects. And there are plenty of monster-size machines to do the job.

Hanz

Dig This!

The **Bagger 288** is the largest vehicle ever to travel on land. It is 311 feet tall, 705 feet long, and weighs 45,500 tons (the weight of the ocean liner *Titanic* was about 46,000 tons). The machine is used to remove dirt or coal from mines. A spinning disc at the end of a long arm is powerful enough to level a mountain.

Incredible!

The Bagger 288 excavator can dig a hole the length of a soccer field and as deep as a seven-story building in one day.

Mighty Movers

NASA, the National Aeronautics and Space Administration, has some heavy objects, such as space shuttles, rockets, and launch platforms. Moving them from one place to another isn't easy. That's why NASA built two crawler-transporters, nicknamed **Hanz** and **Franz**, after two weightlifting characters on a TV comedy show. These vehicles are at the Kennedy Space Center in Cape Canaveral, Florida. Each weighs 6,000,000 pounds. Their top decks are about the size of a baseball infield.

Franz

Incredible!

Since 1977, both crawler-transporters have traveled a combined distance of 1,243 miles—as long as a round trip from the Kennedy Space Center to New York City. It would be a slow trip, because the machines move only one mile per hour when loaded.

Big, Big Bubbles

A bubble is a thin film of material that is filled with air. A bubble can also be a very light, non-solid object that is shaped like a sphere. Bubbles can range in size from tiny, like the ones in soft drinks, to the size of the Milky Way.

Bodacious Bubbles

Using large loops, it's possible to make bubbles so large they can surround a person. One person fit more than 100 people inside a single bubble. Another person created a tube-shaped bubble that was 105 feet long. Perhaps the biggest-ever **free-floating bubble** is shown here. More than 13,600 baseballs could have fit inside it!

Far Out Bubble

The biggest bubbles in the galaxy aren't made from soap or bubble gum: They are made of energy. Two huge space bubbles were discovered by NASA. One bubble extends above the center of the Milky Way and one extends below it. Each bubble is 25,000 light years from one end to the other. A light year—the distance light travels in one year—is equal to nearly six trillion miles. Scientists think the bubbles are made of a vast amount of energy that burst into space. What caused the burst of energy is a big mystery.

BTW!

The Milky Way, the home galaxy of our solar system, is about 100,000 light years across and contains about 2 billion stars.

For the Record

The Topps company created the largest single piece of bubble gum. It was equal to 10,000 pieces of normal-size pieces of Bazooka gum.

Blow Up

Americans like to chew bubble gum. And they like to blow bubbles with the gum. The biggest bubble-gum bubble on record was 23 inches in diameter.

Living Large

Most people don't think of spiders as being large. But the goliath tarantula is nearly a foot across and can eat a bird. There are other jumbo species of animals that are usually on the small side. They are the biggest of the smallest.

Bugging Out

This is one bug you don't want to step on. The six-legged critter is a **giant water bug**, one of the largest insects in the world. Some species are about four and a half inches long–about the length of a toilet paper roll. Giant water bugs eat salamanders, frogs, and even fish twice their size. Smaller species can be found in North America. The jumbo-size ones live in North and South America and in East Asia. If you see one, be careful: they bite!

Incredible!

Giant water bugs are served up as food in Thailand. The nutritious bug contains calcium, protein, and iron.

This rodent's back is really roomy!

Whopper of a Rodent

Rodents are usually fairly small mammals: Think mice, squirrels, and chipmunks. Now think of a rodent the length of a snowboard. That creature is a **capybara** (ka-pee-*bar*-uh), the biggest rodent in the world. Found in South America, it is four feet long, two feet high, and weighs up to 180 pounds. A capybara eats grass and enjoys swimming in marshy water.

Incredible!

A giant clam is a real homebody. When it attaches itself to a reef, the clam stays on that spot for the rest of its life—which can be as long as 100 years.

Clam Up

Most clams are about four inches across. But a monster-size mollusk lurks in the coral reefs of the western Pacific and Indian Oceans. On average, **giant clams** are four feet across and weigh about 440 pounds. The largest one ever found was 734 pounds. Giant clam shells are so large, they have been used as wash basins.

4 feet across!

Give Him a Big Hand

NBA Superstar Shaquille O'Neal's hands are really large! From his wrist to the tip of his middle finger, Shaq's hand is about 9½ inches long. Compare your hand size to his just by putting it on top of this photo.

0 Inch 1

Actual Size

Incredible!

Shaq is 7 feet 1 inch tall and weighs 325 pounds. He has been on 14 NBA All-Star teams and has been an All-NBA selection 13 times. Shaq received the NBA's Most Valuable Player award for the 1999-2000 season.

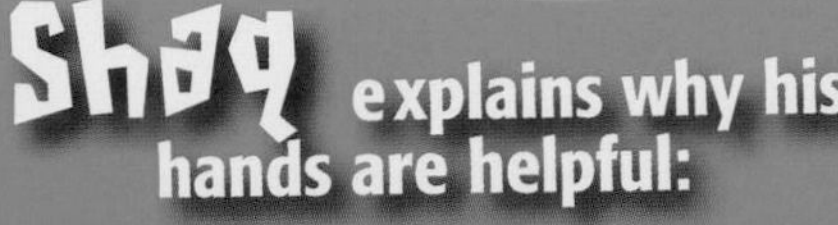

Shaq explains why his hands are helpful:

"My hands are important because I can palm the ball. Besides my overall athletic skill, palming the ball allows me to easily grab rebounds and throw down dunks against my opponents."

For the Record

One of the tallest men on record, Sultan Kosen, is 8 feet 1 inch tall. His hands measure 10.83 inches from wrist to the end of the middle finger. Compare that with the size of your hand.

How tall are you? How do you size up to Kosen and O'Neal?

BTW

Each of your hands contains 29 bones and 34 muscles.

Artists Think Big—and Small

Astonishing artwork comes in all sizes. There are great sculptures hundreds of feet tall carved into a cliff. And there are sensational sculptures made from the tip of a pencil. For artists, no creation can be too big or too small.

Giant Buddha

The Leshan Giant Buddha was carved out of a cliff near the city of Leshan, in China. The world's largest stone Buddha, it was built between 713 and 803. The statue faces a river, and the men who built the statue hoped the Buddha would calm its rough waters. The big Buddha is 233 feet high and is 92 feet wide across the shoulders. Each eyebrow is 18 feet long, and the ears are each 23 feet long. Its feet are 36 feet long, and a person could sit on a toenail.

From TIME FOR KIDS

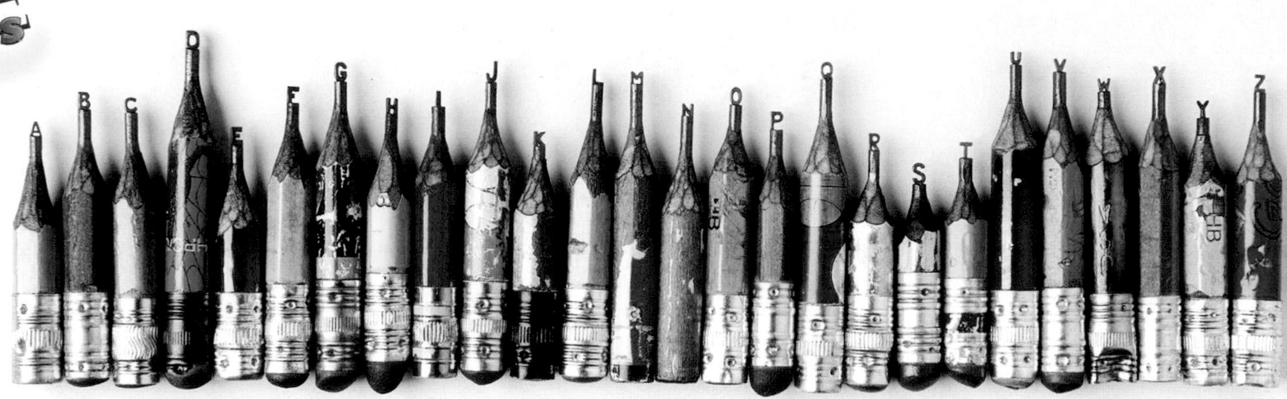

Little Letters

Usually, pencils are used to create art. But for Dalton Ghetti, the pencil *is* the art. Ghetti carves his masterpieces on the pencils' tiny tips, using a sewing needle, a razor blade, and a whole lot of patience. It took him two and a half years to make this **alphabet**. Dalton doesn't use a magnifying glass while carving. (You may need one to view the tiny letters on top of each tip.) He must have great eyesight!

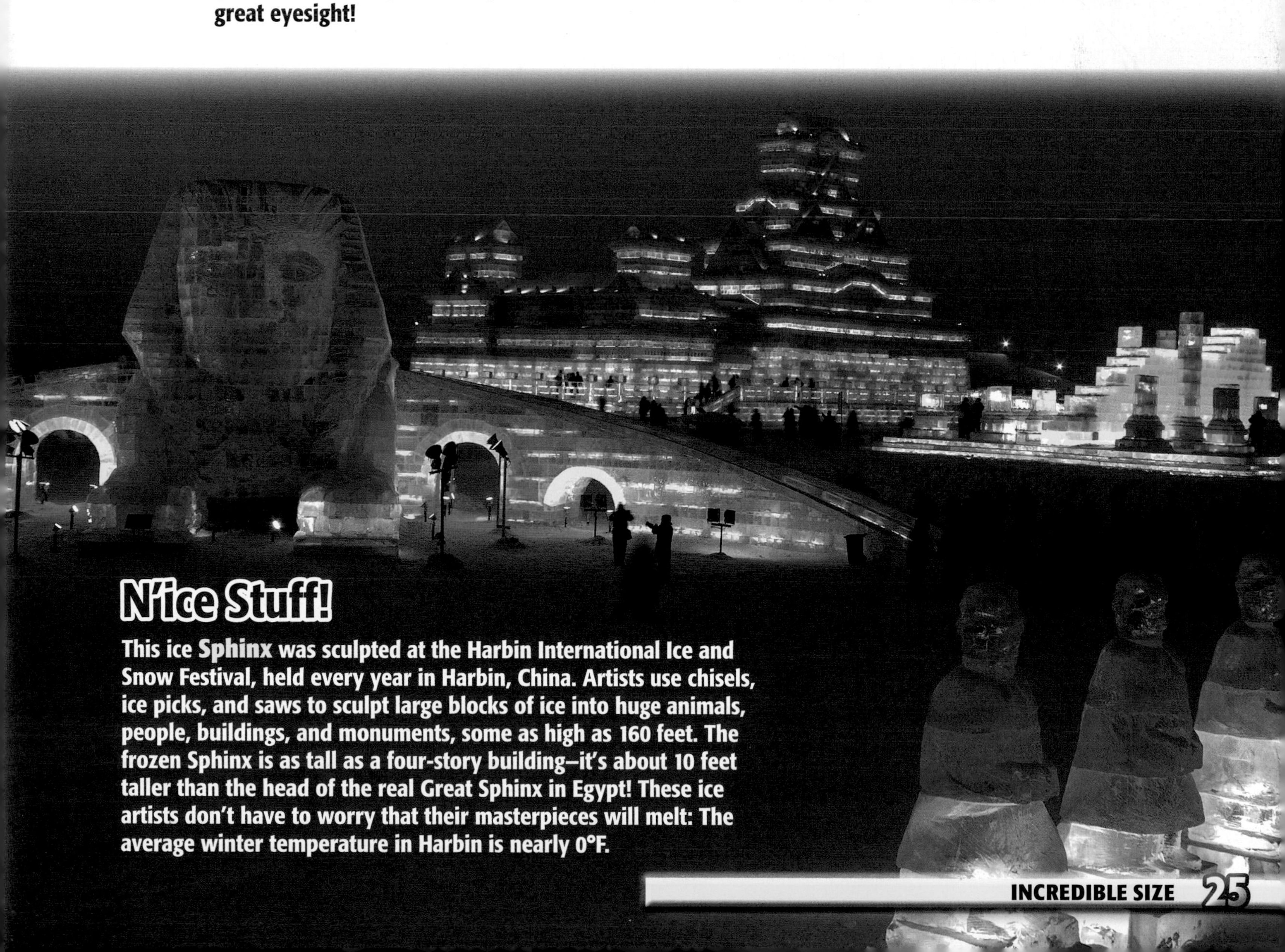

N'ice Stuff!

This ice **Sphinx** was sculpted at the Harbin International Ice and Snow Festival, held every year in Harbin, China. Artists use chisels, ice picks, and saws to sculpt large blocks of ice into huge animals, people, buildings, and monuments, some as high as 160 feet. The frozen Sphinx is as tall as a four-story building—it's about 10 feet taller than the head of the real Great Sphinx in Egypt! These ice artists don't have to worry that their masterpieces will melt: The average winter temperature in Harbin is nearly 0°F.

The Incredible Shrinking White House

If you can't get to the White House, the White House might come to you. This miniature version of the home of the First Family was created by John Zweifel. It took the Wisconsin native 50 years to create an exact copy of the famous house. Even the photos in the Oval Office are the same as the ones President Barack Obama displays. The mini White House has toured every U.S. state.

Most visitors don't get to see the President's bedroom. But Zweifel got special permission to include it in the model.

The President's study has a tiny flat-screen TV that really works.

The Blue Room is the usual place for Presidents to greet guests. Like the actual room, this mini version is decorated with a flower arrangement.

The miniature books in the library are the same ones that are kept in the real White House. Many even have text inside, which can be read with a magnifying glass.

The rugs are, stitch for stitch, exact copies of the originals. Some, like this one in the Diplomatic Reception Room, took years to create.

Zweifel has included such details as the roller-skate marks left on the floor of the East Room by President Jimmy Carter's daughter Amy in 1976. When the White House floor was fixed, Zweifel polished this floor too.

Tens of thousands of volunteers have spent more than 600,000 hours working on the model over the years. A 2½-inch carved table in the Lincoln Bedroom took 160 hours to complete.

To make the model, Zweifel used photos, drawings, and memories from hundreds of visits to the White House.

Incredible!

The mini White House is 60 feet long and 20 feet wide. One inch on the model equals one foot of the real thing.

Look Closely

The White House model is full of tiny details. Some have been added since the Obamas moved in.

This is a hand-painted copy of a picture chosen by the First Lady for the master bedroom.

Each table in the State Dining Room has tiny place settings of official White House china.

An artist who specializes in creating miniature animals made this tiny version of Bo, the Obamas' dog.

Big City, Small Town

For the first time in history, more than 50 percent of Earth's almost seven billion people are city dwellers. Experts think that by 2030, the number of city dwellers will increase to about five billion. Big cities are becoming even bigger. But plenty of people still live in small—sometimes very small—cities and towns.

Tokyo Is Terrific!

Nearly one-fourth of Japan's population lives in or near Tokyo, the nation's capital. That's about 35,600,000 people who manage to squeeze into a fairly small area. Tokyo's streets are crowded, sometimes even at three o'clock in the morning. The subways are also packed, especially at rush hour. About 8 million people ride the subway every day. Getting around the city can be hard, because most streets have no names. And the buildings are numbered not in sequence but in the order they were built. Still, Tokyo's busy, bustling streets make it an exciting city.

No, it's not the Eiffel Tower. Called the **Tokyo Tower**, the 1,091-foot structure holds an antenna that broadcasts radio and TV signals. Visitors can take an elevator to observation decks at the top and see Tokyo spread out below.

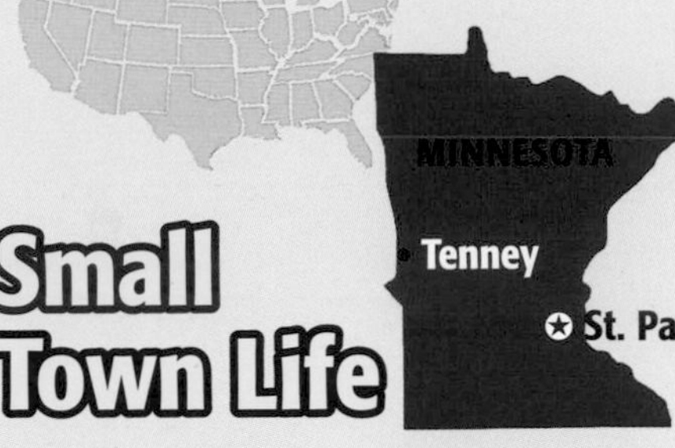

Small Town Life

There might be a smaller city than **Tenney**, but it would be hard to find it. According to the 2000 Census, Tenney, Minnesota, has a population of six. The population actually went down from six to two shortly after the 2000 Census was taken. Tenney had one place to shop: a general store, but it has been out of business for several years. The size of the town is 0.01 square miles, so if you drive by, look quickly or you'll miss it.

Built in 1904, the Tenney Fire Hall once housed the city's two hand-pulled fire engines.

Most Populous U.S. Cities

CITY	POPULATION
1. New York City, NY	8,391,881
2. Los Angeles, CA	3,831,868
3. Chicago, IL	2,851,268
4. Houston, TX	2,257,926
5. Phoenix, AZ	1,593,659

Source: U.S. Census

Good Things Come in Small Packages

Many people like to live in big houses. But small houses are great too. And with them, there's more than meets the eye. Small houses are faster to build, use fewer materials, and can squeeze in just about anywhere. And if the house is really tiny, you can lift it up and take it with you when you move.

The Smallest House IN GREAT BRITAIN
Y TY LLEIAF YM MHRYDAIN FAWR

A Wee House

It's known as the smallest house in Great Britain, and it might be one of the smallest homes anywhere. The Quay House, located in Conwy, Wales, measures 6 feet wide and 10 feet high. It was built in the 1600s, and people lived in it until 1900. The last person who called it home was 6 feet 3 inches tall: He couldn't stand up straight inside the house.

Incredible!

When the Inuit people build houses, they think small. The native people of the Arctic make and live in igloos—homes made of ice and snow. Igloos keep people warm in the winter, but in the summer, the igloos melt away!

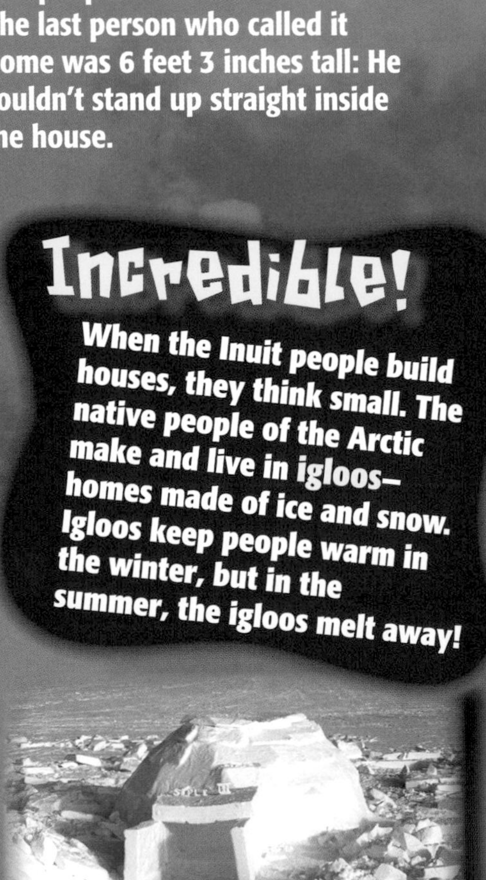

Less Is More

Here's a house that can be delivered by truck to any place you want to live. The **Arado weeHouse** has a bathroom called a weepee. Perfect for one or two people, the home manages to fit two beds, a dining room, a kitchen, entertainment equipment, and a wood-burning fireplace.

A Wheel-y Great Home

The tiny **QTvan** can fit a bed, bookshelves, a widescreen TV—and one person. The home travels at a top speed of six miles per hour and can be hooked up to an electrical outlet when it stops for the night. Owners can add a satellite dish so they can get plenty of TV channels.

Chapter 2
Incredible Animals and Plants

Humans share the planet with countless numbers of living things, from the smallest one-celled funguses to mammoth whales and towering redwood trees. Plants and animals make their homes in mountains, deserts, underground, and at the bottom of the oceans. To survive in these different conditions, organisms have come up with endless and fascinating ways of staying alive.

In This Chapter

- Blood-Sucking Animals
- Dragons on the Loose
- Some High I.Q. Critters
- Stinkiest Plants Ever
- Curious-Looking Cats
- Long-Lived Living Things
- Amazing Frogs

And Much More!

This flower can reach up to 5 times my height!

For the Record

The **corpse flower** is one of the few plants that can produce its own heat. The high temperature sends its stinky smell farther, attracting more insects.

BTW

A Komodo dragon has an excellent sense of smell. The dragon's tongue flicks out to taste the air, picking up the scent of prey from as far away as five miles.

Incredible!

About 70 percent of all known species of living things can be found in 11 countries: Australia, Brazil, China, Colombia, Ecuador, India, Indonesia, Madagascar, Mexico, Peru, and the Democratic Republic of The Congo.

MEXICO
COLOMBIA
ECUADOR
PERU
BRAZIL
DEMOCRATIC REPUBLIC OF THE CONGO
MADAGASCAR
CHINA
INDIA
INDONESIA
AUSTRALIA

Introducing... New Animals

There are between 2 and 50 million species of plants and animals on Earth. So far, only about 1.7 million different types of living things (not counting one-celled life, such as bacteria) have been discovered. But each year experts find about **10,000** new species. Whether found on land or water, many of these newly discovered species are truly astonishing!

Count Frog-ula

The **vampire flying frog** sounds like one scary amphibian! But the recently discovered frog doesn't really fly and doesn't suck blood. The two-inch-long croaker has webs between its toes and fingers. These let it glide from tree to tree in the forests of southern Vietnam, a country in Southeast Asia. The frog got the vampire name because its tadpoles have tiny fangs (shown below). Scientists think the **little black fangs** might be used to cut up food or to grip objects—but not to drink **blood**!

Hairy Crab

Discovered on the floor of the South Pacific Ocean, the **yeti crab** is covered with strands of hair-like bristles. Experts think the hair may collect bacteria that the crab eats. Or the bacteria might clean dangerous minerals found in the water the crabs live in.

Give Me a Hand

The **pink handfish** looks like it can give high fives. But its "hands" are actually fins that the fish uses to walk along the ocean floor. This four-inch-long fish was found along the coast of Australia. There are 14 species of these handy fish, but nine of them are endangered.

Animal Suckers

Some animals will eat just about anything, from plants to meat. More picky animals eat only plants or only meat. Then there are critters who make a meal of blood—sometimes human blood.

Blood Thirsty

The **lamprey** is one freaky-looking bloodsucker! This eel-like fish has no jaw—but it does have a mouth with suckers and sharp teeth. The lamprey uses both to clamp onto a fish. Then the lamprey's rough tongue scrapes off the skin of its victim until it bleeds. The lamprey produces a chemical that stops blood from clotting, so the fish can drink blood for hours, days, or even weeks—until it's full or its prey dies.

Tick, Tock

A **tick** hangs around on grass or trees, waiting for an animal (or person) to brush against it. The bug then hops aboard, finds a warm, moist spot, and feasts on its host's blood with its sharp mouthparts. When full, the tick drops onto the ground.

For the Record

The tick's body gets bigger as it fills with blood, sometimes as much as **100 times** its bodyweight.

Count Bat-cula

Vampire bats can fit in the palm of your hand—but you might not want to hold one. Native to Mexico and Central and South America, the flying mammal lands near its victims—usually cattle and horses, but sometimes humans—before cautiously climbing on them. After its razor-sharp front teeth slice open the skin, the bat's tongue slurps up blood flowing from the wound.

A Worm's-Eye View

Leeches are worms that hang out in wet places, such as ponds and lakes. One type of leech sticks a hollow needle into an animal to drink its blood. Another type has three jaws that slice into an animal. The leech produces a chemical so the animal doesn't feel pain. That way, the victim isn't aware it has become a meal, and the leech can feast in peace.

Blast from the Past

In earlier centuries, people believed that disease could be cured by removing blood from the body. So, doctors performed bloodlettings—they caused people to bleed. In medieval times, doctors sometimes put leeches on parts of the body to remove blood.

Funny Faces

Tigers, dolphins, horses…many animals seem beautiful to humans. But some critters have features that look a bit strange to us. As odd as those features might appear, they have a purpose. Their strange-looking parts make it possible for the animal to stay alive.

The Nose Knows

The star-nosed mole can't see very well. To find food, it uses a chunk of skin on its nose that has 22 separate tentacles, or feelers. These tentacles are incredibly sensitive to touch—five times more so than human fingertips. The mole uses them almost like a cat uses whiskers. They let the mole feel its way around and find tiny animals to eat.

Incredible!

The star-nosed mole eats faster than any other mammal in the world. It can wolf down a meal in 227 milliseconds—less time than it takes for a person to glance at a flash of light.

Head Case

A hammerhead shark doesn't pound nails. But its hammer-shaped head is useful. Because the shark's eyes are so far apart, its sight has greater range than other sharks. Its nostrils are also separated, letting it smell a larger area. Some researchers think the shark might use the head to help steer through the water—like a rudder on a ship. Or it may use the head like a paddle to help it dive deep.

Helmet Head

A **cassowary** is a flightless bird. It gets from here to there by running through bushes and around trees in the rainforests of Australia. Standing six feet tall, it often bumps its head against branches. That's when the bony shield on the top of its head comes in handy. The helmet keeps the bird from getting brained by the branches.

For the Record

The second largest bird in the world, a cassowary can weigh up to 128 pounds. Although it can't fly, it can run as fast as 30 miles per hour and jump five feet in the air.

Old Timers

It would be hard to fit candles on the birthday cake of some living things. The average life span of a human in the U.S. is about 77. But some species of animals can live twice as long. Trying to figure out the life span of animals is no easy task. (Some animals outlive the researchers.) But scientists have come up with what they think are the accurate ages of some very long-lived animals—and plants.

A Whale of a Life

At one time, humans were thought to be the longest-living mammals, but no longer. That honor goes to the **bowhead whale**. Researchers claim that one bowhead was 211 years old when it died. Other bowhead whales lived to be 135, 159, and 172 years.

211 YEARS OLD!

Pining Away

In the Great Basin National Park in Nevada, a scientist cut down a **bristlecone pine** tree and discovered it was nearly 5,000 years old. Today, another bristlecone pine, called Methuselah (named after a very old person in the Bible), grows in a secret place in California's White Mountains. The location is secret so no one will harm the tree. It is more than 4,600 years old, making it the oldest tree in the world.

For the Record

The longest-lived insect is the termite queen: It can live up to **50 years**. Some species of queen ants live for nearly 30 years.

A Fishy Story

100 YEARS OLD!

The European sturgeon is an ancient fish, and it looks like one. In fact, it hasn't changed much since its ancestors first took to the water 65 million years ago. The fish can live up to 100 years. These fish are very rare and very endangered.

Incredible!

The longest-lived life-form on the planet may be a strain of bacteria found below the earth in Carlsbad, New Mexico. Scientists claim the bacteria are 250 million years old. The single-celled life was dormant, or inactive, until scientists brought them back to life.

A Living Fossil

The **tuatara** is one strange creature. It looks like a lizard, but it's actually related to a group of extinct reptiles that lived during the age of the dinosaurs. A tuatara can move quickly, but practically everything else about it is slow. The reptile doesn't reach its full length until it's 30 years old. And it can go an hour without breathing if necessary. Maybe that's why tuataras in the wild have a life span of up to 80 years.

80 YEARS OLD!

A Dragon's Tale

There are more than 3,000 types of lizards. The largest and deadliest of them all is the Komodo dragon. Although the Komodo doesn't breathe fire, it is one very scary reptile!

Komodo dragons can run as fast as 13 miles an hour. Still, a dragon likes to catch a meal by quietly waiting for prey to pass by. The dragon then uses its powerful claws and sharp teeth to kill its victim. If the animal manages to get away, the dragon isn't worried. A Komodo's bite contains deadly poison. And if the poison doesn't work, bacteria in a dragon's saliva will infect the prey and kill it. All the Komodo has to do is follow the animal and wait for it to die.

Night Stalkers

Komodo dragons, like this baby getting a ride on its mother's back, are only found on several islands in Komodo National Park, in the Asian nation of Indonesia. Except in one fishing village on Komodo, no humans live on the islands. Villagers build their homes on stilts, and don't go out in the evenings when the dragons are active. Still, the people like the dragons because they bring in tourists. And tourists spend money, which helps support the villagers.

Blast from the Past

Komodo dragons were first discovered around 1911. That's when an airplane pilot was forced down and swam to Komodo Island. There, he found the dragons and lived to tell the tale.

Dragons are big—they average about nine feet long and 200 pounds—and they have a big appetite. In one sitting, a hungry Komodo can eat 80 percent of its body weight. These reptiles will devour just about anything, from wild pigs and deer to water buffalos and any human who isn't careful.

For the Record

The largest Komodo dragon on record—and so the largest lizard in the world—measured more than 10 feet long and weighed 366 pounds. But the largest reptile in the world is the saltwater crocodile, which can reach about 20 feet in length.

Great Performances

Many animals are great actors, but their best roles aren't in movies. The top animal actors perform in the wild–and they do it in order to survive. Some animal actors use natural disguises to look (and sometimes act) like a different animal. Others change their shape to confuse enemies. If animals are successful in their roles, they don't get applause–they get to live another day.

Giving Blood

The **Texas horned lizard** is a master of special effects. When threatened by a large predator, such as a fox or dog, the reptile plays a character in a horror movie: It squirts blood out of its eyes. The disgusting-tasting blood can travel up to six feet. This gory feat is enough to frighten just about any animal. The lizard doesn't perform the act very often, because it uses up about 25 percent of its blood.

What a Hoot!

One insect often turns its back to an audience. The front of the **owl butterfly** is a beautiful blue. But the back of its wings looks like brown feathers. On the "feathers" are two yellow spots that resemble an owl's eyes. When the wings are stretched, the back of the butterfly looks to its enemies like an owl's head. Many birds that eat butterflies fear owls, so they keep their distance.

Whoooo's trying to look like me?

Playing Possum

The **Virginia (or North American) opossum** puts its acting skills to the test when cornered by an enemy. That's when this marsupial (an animal whose young develops in the mother's pouch) "plays dead." The Virginia opossum falls down and lies on the ground with its mouth and its glassy eyes open. If the performance works, the predator leaves the opossum for another victim. Take a bow!

Not to worry, I'm just pretending!

For the Record

The Virginia opossum is the only marsupial north of Mexico.

Frills and Chills

Some animals startle their enemies, which gives them time to flee. One such animal is the **frilled lizard**. When frightened, it opens a flap of skin around its neck that looks like a big collar. The lizard hopes it will freak out its foe.

BTW

If the frill doesn't scare away enemies, the lizard will flee. When running away, it uses just its back legs. That's why it got the nickname "bicycle lizard."

Cool Cats

Cats are curious creatures. And some of them are curious looking. There are many breeds of cats, so these critters come in all kinds of colors and patterns. They also grow different lengths and types of hair, tails, and ears. Some of the most unusual breeds of cats take center stage at cat shows. That's where you're more likely to see these fabulous felines.

Weight a Minute!

The heavyweight champ of felines is the **Maine coon**. It can weigh up to 30 pounds and grows as long as 40 inches. The cat's long bushy tail may have fooled some people into thinking it was part raccoon, or 'coon. The huge cat has shaggy fur and big feet, so it has no trouble walking on snow or ice. The cats may have first appeared in Turkey, but they love the cold weather of their adopted home, Maine.

Short Stuff

Named after the little people in *The Wizard of Oz*, **munchkins** have short, stumpy legs that are about half the size of a normal cat's legs. Like a dachshund, these sausage-shaped cats like to walk on a leash and are friendly and playful.

For the Record

Cats are the most popular house pet, with about 90 million of them in nearly one-third of American homes.

Get an Earful

American curl cats are "ear-y." At birth, their ears are straight. But after a few days, the ears begin to curl towards the back of the cat. After a few months, the ears stop curling. The first curl cats were found in California in 1981, and since then they have been bred all over the world.

Going Bald

Bald and wrinkled, the **sphynx** (sfinks) is a rare cat. Although it seems to be hairless, the cat does have short, fine fur on parts of its body. Without thick fur to keep it warm, the sphynx needs to snuggle up to other cats or humans. These bare-bodied cats can also get sunburned.

Blast from the Past

Cats and humans have been partners for a long time. Some scientists think cats were first domesticated, or tamed, in the Near East about 12,000 years ago. Cats became important to humans because they killed rodents that ate grain in storehouses.

Incredible!

A cat has whiskers on many parts of its body—not just its face. The whiskers let the cat feel objects in the dark.

Disappearing Acts

Soldiers wear camouflage uniforms to help them blend into their surroundings. That way, the enemy won't see them. Many animals use natural camouflage to either hide from enemies or sneak up on them unnoticed. An animal's color or pattern allows it to blend into the background.

A Colorful Character

The **cuttlefish** isn't a fish—it's a mollusk, like squids and octopuses. Pigments under its skin produce many colors and patterns, so it can blend in almost anywhere. The creature can even change the texture of its skin from smooth to bumpy to spiky to imitate its surroundings—all in a matter of seconds.

Incredible!

The **cuttlefish** squirts out a reddish-brown ink when threatened. In the past, that ink has been used by artists to draw and paint a color called sepia (*see*-pea-uh).

Looks Like Lichen

A katydid is a winged insect that looks like a grasshopper. The **lichen katydid** lives in tropical cloud forests in Central America and hides out among lichen plants. Lichens have tangled fibers, and the katydid's body perfectly matches the complicated patterns of the leaves.

Beautiful but Deadly

In Central and South America, the eyelash viper hangs out on the branches of fruit trees, or near flowers. Its bright color lets the snake disappear into the background. When prey gets close, the poisonous snake strikes. The viper also has scales over its eyes that stick out like eyelashes. They make its head look more like the plants around it.

Blast from the Past

Some eyelash vipers are a very bright yellow. Because of the snake's golden color and dangerous bite, early explorers of Central America called it "false gold."

Rock On

Some animals have features that look like stones and pebbles. This makes it possible for the creatures to hide. One of the best rock camouflages belongs to the scorpion fish. Its thick ridges and spines make it look like coral or a chunk of rock covered by sand. It can even change its color to blend in better with the background. Some types of scorpion fish will sway from side to side like a piece of debris shifting in the currents.

Mixed-Up Animals

In the animal kingdom, creatures of two different species usually don't mate. But when they do, they sometimes create an entirely new species called a hybrid. For example, a mule is a combination of a donkey and a horse. Sometimes different species mate in the wild. People have bred two different species to create a hybrid in captivity. The resulting hybrid may turn out to be an incredible mix of its parents.

Horse of a Different Color

A zebroid is an animal that's half zebra and half some other member of the horse family. A zorse is half horse and half zebra. A **zonkey** is half donkey and half zebra. Combine a zebra and a female pony and you get a zony. Zebroids are usually smaller than a normal horse, and they have stripes on part of their body. Zebroids can be ridden like a horse, but are stronger.

Marine Mammal Mix-Up

The **wholphin** is part bottlenose dolphin and part false killer whale. Two wholphins exist in the Sea Life Park in Hawaii. The blend between the two parents even shows up in its teeth. Bottlenose dolphins have 88 teeth, while false killer whales have 44. The first wholphin bred in captivity, named Kekaimalu, had 66 teeth.

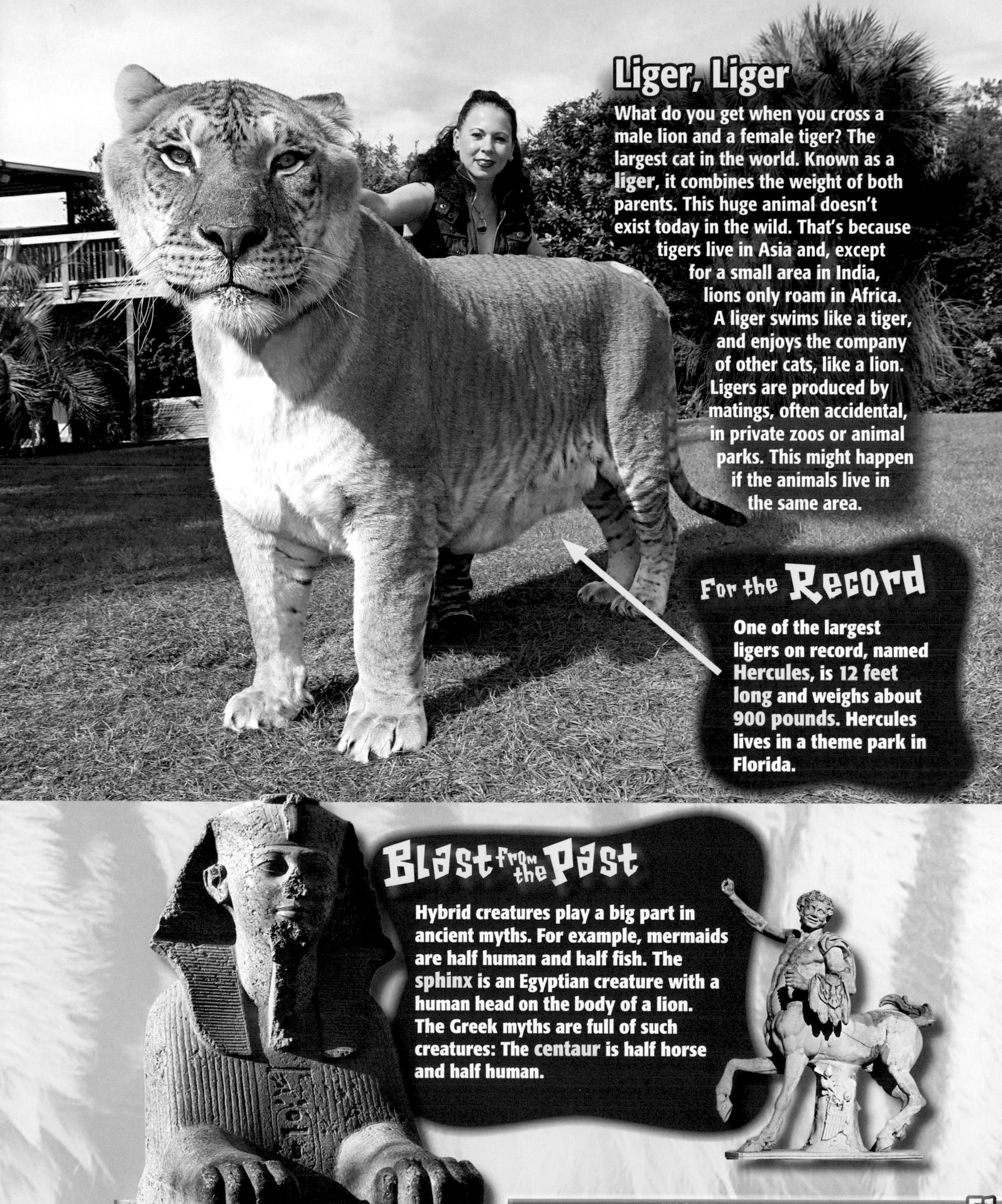

Liger, Liger

What do you get when you cross a male lion and a female tiger? The largest cat in the world. Known as a **liger**, it combines the weight of both parents. This huge animal doesn't exist today in the wild. That's because tigers live in Asia and, except for a small area in India, lions only roam in Africa. A liger swims like a tiger, and enjoys the company of other cats, like a lion. Ligers are produced by matings, often accidental, in private zoos or animal parks. This might happen if the animals live in the same area.

For the Record

One of the largest ligers on record, named Hercules, is 12 feet long and weighs about 900 pounds. Hercules lives in a theme park in Florida.

Blast from the Past

Hybrid creatures play a big part in ancient myths. For example, mermaids are half human and half fish. The **sphinx** is an Egyptian creature with a human head on the body of a lion. The Greek myths are full of such creatures: The **centaur** is half horse and half human.

Creating a Stink

Many flowers produce sweet smells that attract insects and animals. When these creatures come into contact with the flowers, pollen often sticks to them. The animals then transfer the pollen to other plants, which grow new plants. But there are some flowers you'd never give anyone on St. Valentine's Day. That's because they give off a terrible odor—terrible to humans, that is.

Hold Your Nose!

Found in Southeast Asia, the rafflesia (ra-*fleazh*-uh) plant starts off looking like a lump. Nine months later, it grows to the size of a basketball. Finally, its monstrously huge flowers open. They can be up to three feet in diameter and weigh more than 20 pounds. The flowers give off a horrible smell that some have called worse than that of rotting flesh.

Skunk Funk

The skunk cabbage, also known as skunkweed and polecatweed, grows near ponds, streams, and other wet areas. When it blooms, the flowers look like something out of a horror movie. And its leaves smell like something from a horror movie, too—a revolting odor. In some indoor gardens, the plant grows near an exit so grossed-out visitors can leave in a hurry.

BTW

Why are some plants stinky? One reason is to keep away plant-eating animals that might want to chew on them. More importantly, the horrible smell attracts flies, dung beetles, and other insects that are lured by the odor of rotten meat. They fly or crawl onto the plants, and as they do, they pick up pollen. They take this pollen to other stinky plants. When the pollen falls off, it fertilizes that plant. Soon there will be new smelly plants growing.

Big Smell

The name of this flower tells you everything: corpse flower. The flower is native to the country of Indonesia. Some people say the flower smells like poop, others say it stinks like something dead. Luckily, fewer than 30 of them have ever bloomed in the U.S.

For the Record

The corpse flower is one of the largest flowers in the world. In the wild it can grow up to 10 feet tall and five feet across.

Animal Smarts

How smart are animals? Scientists (and pet owners) have argued over this question for a long time. Today, more and more research seems to show that some types of animals have intelligence. Researchers are discovering that humans aren't the only animals that can use language or tools.

Nutty Behavior

In an experiment, a bird called a western scrub jay hid a nut in sight of another jay. Later when the bird was gone, the jay that hid the nut came back and moved the food. Scientists claim the bird realized the other bird might steal its nut. Researchers say the jay was capable of stealing nuts and was intelligent enough to know that the other bird would act just as badly.

Brainy Dolphins

To see just how smart dolphins are, scientists tried to communicate with several dolphins in captivity. Researchers made a sign language of hand and arm movements and taught it to the dolphins. When the scientists made a gesture, the dolphins would react to it. For example, if the human moved both arms to indicate "hoop, ball, fetch," the dolphin would correctly push a ball to a hoop. The dolphins learned the language almost immediately. They also obeyed the signals given by a person on an underwater TV screen. The dolphins understood that the person on the screen was a real person. So how smart are dolphins? Very.

How Smart Is Your Dog?

What You Need

An empty can
A doggy treat
A stopwatch

What to Do

1. Show your dog the treat and let it sniff it.
2. While your pet watches you, place the treat on the floor. Cover it with the empty can.
3. Start the stopwatch and encourage your dog to knock over the can and get the treat.

Scoring

Rate your dog using this scale. If your dog got the snack in…

- **5 seconds or less:** Canine genius
- **5 to 15 seconds:** Doggy brainiac
- **15 to 30 seconds:** Very smart dog
- **30 to 60 seconds:** An average pooch
- **Tries but can't get the treat:** This dog isn't learning new tricks
- **Doesn't try to get it:** Still, a nice pet

From TIME FOR KIDS

A Great Ape

Kanzi is a bonobo that lives in an ape research center in Des Moines, Iowa. Bonobos are close cousins of the chimp. Kanzi and six other bonobos have been raised from birth with both spoken language and symbols as part of each day.

Researchers have taught Kanzi more than 384 words. He uses colorful sheets showing symbols that stand for words. He knows words that stand for objects, such as noodles, tummy, bowl, and candy. And he also understands words that represent ideas and emotions, such as good, bad, now, and happy. Kanzi can build thoughts and sentences by pointing at the sheets. Sue Savage-Rumbaugh is a primatologist at the research center. (A primatologist studies primates–animals that include monkeys and apes.) She makes sure researchers don't accidentally give Kanzi clues about words. So, she has someone in another room say a word, and Kanzi hears it through earphones. Kanzi then points to the symbol for the word.

Sign Language

Researchers learned about Kanzi's gift for language by accident. They were trying to teach his mother words and symbols. Young Kanzi was just hanging out near her. Later, Kanzi on his own asked for food by pointing to the symbols for it. Unlike other apes who had been taught to communicate by getting rewards, Kanzi learned like a human child: By listening to adults speak. Soon, Kanzi was able to communicate about objects that weren't within sight. He could understand sentences made with words he had learned.

Kanzi doesn't spend all his time on English lessons. He and the other bonobos get to relax evenings by gobbling down fruit and vegetables while watching DVDs. Some of their favorite movies are *Quest for Fire* and *Every Which Way But Loose*. The stars of the movies are apes.

The bonobos in Iowa know at least **384** words. This chart shows how they create new words using symbols they know.

Slow + Lettuce = Kale
It takes a long time to chew the leafy green vegetable. So Kanzi gave it this name.

Big + Water = Flood
There were floods where Kanzi lives in Iowa. This is how the apes described what they had seen.

Bread + Cheese + Tomato = Pizza
The bonobos like pizza. This is how they ask for it.

Top Pops

In the animal kingdom, parents don't always stick around to raise their offspring. For example, most types of fish swim away before their eggs have hatched. Many species of reptiles and insect babies are on their own at birth. When an animal does raise its young, it's usually the mother who feeds and protects it. But there are some special dads who help take care of their babies.

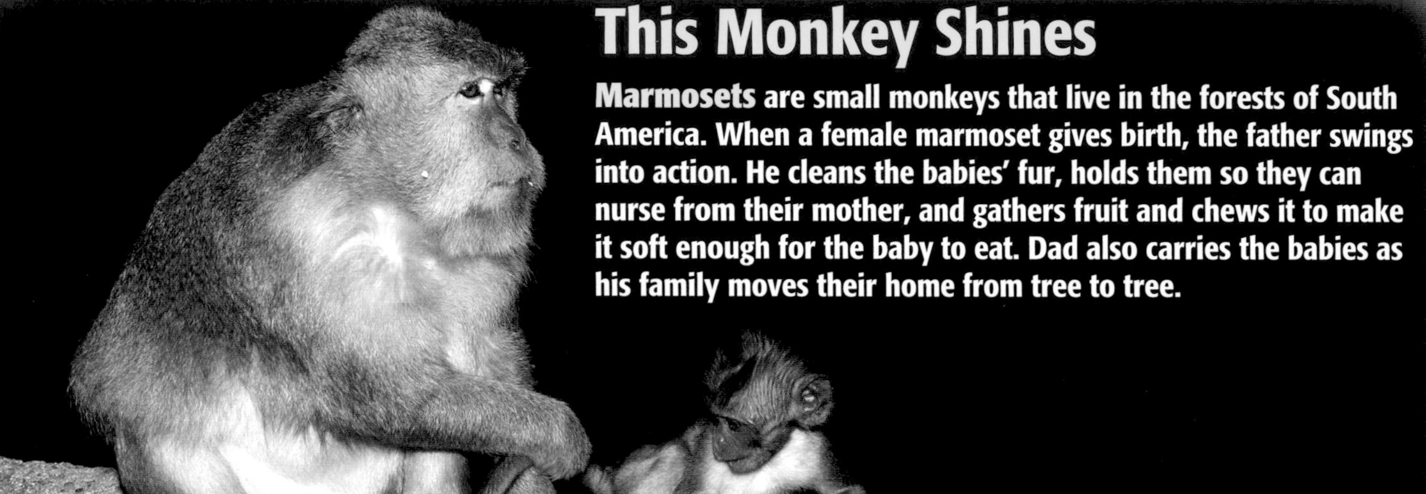

This Monkey Shines

Marmosets are small monkeys that live in the forests of South America. When a female marmoset gives birth, the father swings into action. He cleans the babies' fur, holds them so they can nurse from their mother, and gathers fruit and chews it to make it soft enough for the baby to eat. Dad also carries the babies as his family moves their home from tree to tree.

Sea-ing Is Believing

The male **seahorse** really delivers as a dad. The female seahorse places her eggs in a pouch in the father's stomach and swims away. Dad fertilizes the eggs, and during the next several weeks, the baby seahorses grow inside their father. When they can live on their own, the father pushes the babies out and into the water.

Incredible!

The fin on the back of the seahorse moves back and forth 35 times a second, sending the seahorse forward.

For the Record

Emperor penguins are the largest penguins in the world.

Incredible!

By the time the female penguin shows up to take care of junior, the male has lost about one-third of its body weight.

Emperor of Eggs

Few dads of any species take as big a hand–or foot–in caring for offspring as the **emperor penguin**. They live in Antarctica, where temperatures can drop to -80°F. The female emperor penguin lays one egg a year during the coldest days of winter. Soon after, she passes the egg onto the feet of the father, taking care not to let it touch the freezing ice. The female then takes off into the sea. The male is left behind, balancing the precious egg in a flap of skin on top of its feet.

A male emperor penguin warms an egg by covering it with the feathers around its stomach. For two months, the dads stand together in the ice, huddling together to keep themselves and the eggs warm. By the beginning of summer, the egg hatches.

A father penguin takes care of a just-born baby and feeds it by vomiting up liquid. Soon, mom returns and takes over from dad.

Road Trips

Some animals never travel during their lifetime. Others take long journeys, called migrations. These animals, known as migrants, travel to find food, to mate, or to escape harsh weather. Some animals migrate twice a year. Others might travel twice in a lifetime. The migrations usually occur at the same time each year and are made to the same place. Some animals, especially birds, migrate many thousands of miles.

The Arctic
GREENLAND
Bering Sea
CANADA
Baja California
MEXICO

Whale of a Trip

Every summer, gray whales travel in search of food. The whales swim from the waters off Baja California, up the west coast of the U.S. and Canada to the Bering Sea, between Alaska and Russia. Some swim as far north as the Arctic Ocean. Here, the eating is good, with plankton, a tiny form of sea life, the main meal. This round trip is about 12,000 miles, which makes it one of the longest migrations of any mammal.

Raining Monarchs

Each August, millions of monarch butterflies begin to migrate from Canada and the northern U.S. to spend the winter in Mexico or California. They travel as far as 2,000 miles, sometimes flying 100 miles in a day, to escape the cold. Monarchs produce offspring that will fly back north. But the adults have a short life span, so for them it's a one-way trip.

One Good Tern

The king of long-distance migrants is the Arctic tern. Each year, these birds fly nearly 45,000 miles. The trip takes them from the northern tip of Greenland, where they breed, to the shores of Antarctica and back again. That's equal to 60 trips around the Earth in the bird's lifetime.

Feeling Crabby

One of the shortest migrations takes place on Christmas Island, a territory of Australia. Each year, millions of migrate about three to five miles over five days. They travel from a rain forest to the sea to mate and lay eggs. When the eggs hatch, the babies travel back to the rain forests. The trek is dangerous, because the crabs must cross busy roads and can be run over by cars.

Longest Land-Mammal Migrations

Some land mammals migrate in search of food or better weather. Here are the longest average roundtrips.

1. Barren-ground caribou
2,706 miles*
(Arctic Refuge, Alaska)

2. Wildebeest
498 miles
(Serengeti, Tanzania)

3. Wolf
462 miles
(Bathurst region, Canada)

4. White-eared kob
435 miles
(Sudd region, Sudan)

5. Dhiru
373 miles
(Chang Tang, China)

* Numbers are based on animals living in the regions named

Incredible!

The monarch butterfly's main meal is milkwood leaves. Milkwood is poisonous, which makes the monarch poisonous as well. So, predators leave the butterflies alone.

Amazing Frogs

There are about 6,000 species of amphibians–animals that live in water and on land. About one-third of them are endangered. Frogs and toads make up nearly 90 percent of all amphibians. Many frog species have disappeared entirely because of habitat destruction, pollution, climate change, and disease. Still, there are many amazing croakers around, and new species are still being discovered.

Incredible!

For such a small animal, frogs play an important role in nature. Experts study frogs and other amphibians for early warning signs of damage to the environment. Their thin, porous skin makes them sensitive to changes in their surroundings.

Green Gliders

The flying frogs of Southeast Asia can't fly. But they can glide between trees in the rain forest. The frogs have big fingers and toes that are connected by webs of skin. The frogs also have flaps of skin that stick out from their legs. Together, the webbing and flaps act like parachutes that slow their fall.

Big Boy

The **goliath frog** of West Africa is the world's biggest frog, weighing in at about seven pounds. Its body can reach almost a foot in length, and its legs are about three feet long. The goliath also has big hops: It can leap 10 feet. These frogs can live up to 15 years, eating a diet of crabs, insects, and other frogs.

Little Leaper

Recently discovered in Haiti, the **Macaya breast-spot frog** is one of the smallest frogs in the world. When fully grown, the frog is about the size of a green grape. Unfortunately, this little creature is nearly extinct.

Breath-Taking Discovery

The **aquatic brown frog** was found in a remote part of Borneo, an island that is part of the Asian nation of Indonesia. The unusual creature is the world's first known lungless frog: It breathes just through its skin. Scientists think the frog developed without lungs to survive in mountain rivers, where it lives. Without lungs, the frog doesn't float in water, and so avoids being swept along by the river current.

Chapter 3

Incredible Sports

The feats of victorious athletes fascinate us. We also get a kick out of some of their goofs. But as much as we love to watch sports, we also love to play them. And some of the games people play—from stacking cups to polo on bicycles—are also pretty funny.

In This Chapter

- Blunders and Bloopers
- Unbeatable Records
- Extreme Snowmobiling
- Pros and Their Pets

And Much More!

Incredible!

In extreme snowmobiling, some contestants dangle upside down from the machine, or do somersaults in mid-air, landing right-side up. Others might try a back flip. The more exciting the trick, the better the score—and the more oohs and aahs from the crowd.

Incredible!

Parkour is a great sport for people who find jogging boring. Participants run along a route and try to get past obstacles, such as walls or fences, any way they can—from climbing and leaping to vaulting. The goal of the sport is to show skill while overcoming challenges.

For the Record

Roy Halladay is one of the best pitchers in Major League Baseball. While playing for the Philadelphia Phillies, he won the National League Cy Young Award. He has also pitched two no-hitters, including a perfect game. Hitting against Halladay is no holiday!

All-Time Record Breakers

There's a saying that records are made to be broken. But some sports feats are so incredible they may never be bested.

He's Driven

Richard Petty is called "The King" for good reason. He was the greatest NASCAR racer of all time. Petty won **200 races** during his career, including 27 races in one season, 1967. To get an idea of his domination, the second all-time winner on the NASCAR list, David Pearson, has 105 wins.

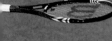

Can't Match This!

The longest tennis match in history took place at the 2010 Wimbledon Championships, in England. The match between **Nicolas Mahut** and **John Isner** took **11 hours and 5 minutes** to complete. The total number of games played was 183, and the last set alone was **138 games (70-68)** and lasted 8 hours and 11 minutes. These are all records.

Oh, Yes!

What professional baseball player owns the record for most lifetime home runs? Babe Ruth? No. Barry Bonds? Wrong again. Bonds holds the Major League record at 762 dingers. But the world record belongs to Japan's **Sadaharu Oh**, who played 22 seasons (1959–1980) for the Yomiuri Giants, in Japan. He hit a total of **868 homers.**

Sadaharu Oh (above) is up at bat against the Baltimore Orioles in a spring training game in 1971. When he was 70, Oh (left) showed that he could still swing a bat.

Masked Marvels

Most people wear masks only on Halloween. But some athletes wear masks when they're on the job: A baseball catcher wears a mask, and so does a football player. Those masks are boring compared to the incredible-looking masks worn by professional ice hockey goalies and pro wrestlers in Mexico. Their marvelous masks express the athletes' personalities.

Where This Buffalo Roams

Ryan Miller, of the Buffalo Sabres, likes lots of details on his mask. The front shows a stylized buffalo, with two crossed sabres (a type of sword) on the chin. On the back, the words Matt Man are a tribute to Miller's cousin Matt, who died of cancer. Matt loved bulldogs, and that's why there's a bulldog wearing the colors of Michigan State University, where Miller went to college. Behind the bulldog is a tree that's a logo for The Steadfast Foundation, a group Miller started to help cancer patients and their families. Miller Time is a play on Miller's name that started when he was in Pee-Wee hockey.

Sabres

Hello, Columbus

Steve Mason is a goaltender for the Columbus Blue Jackets. He grew up in Canada, but the pictures on his masks have to do with his new home, Columbus, Ohio. Mason, like all goalies, wears several different masks during the season. One of the masks (photo, left) shows a picture of Abraham Lincoln. Honest Abe gave speeches in Columbus before and after being elected President in 1860. On the chin is the Ohio state flag. Many of Mason's masks, like the one he wore for the 2011 season (pictured right), have the word Mase–Mason's nickname–on the chin.

Wrestling Cover Up

Pro wrestling is even more popular in Mexico than it is in the U.S. Wrestling in Mexico is called **lucha libre**, or free fighting. A luchador (wrestler) almost always wears a colorfully designed mask that shows an animal, god, ancient hero, or other image. The wrestler is known by his or her mask, like a superhero. The athletes not only wrestle in the masks, they often wear them outside the ring in public.

Strange Sports

Basketball, soccer, and skateboarding are popular sports. Millions of people enjoy playing and watching them. But there are plenty of other fun sports that are lesser known. They may seem a bit odd, but not to the people who take part in them.

Overcoming Obstacles

The world is an obstacle course. That's the idea behind a sport called **parkour** (*parr*-core). People who practice parkour don't run around objects in their way. Instead they jump, crawl, vault, or climb over them. Each person can create his or her own moves to get over walls, fences, railings, rocks, trees, holes in the ground, and other obstacles. The sport can be as easy as running up stairs or as difficult as climbing a tree. It's all about doing your best and challenging yourself. Of course, no one should try parkour without proper training and instruction.

Stacktacular

Sport stacking moves so fast, it's hard to tell what's happening. Players arrange 12 lightweight plastic cups by building pyramids and breaking them down in a particular order. There are age divisions from 4 years and younger to 60 years. Who are the best at this sport? Here's how it stacks up: The fastest stackers are kids in the 11-year-old division.

BTW

A study claims that cup stacking improves hand-eye coordination and reaction time up to 30 percent.

Having a Ball

If riding a bike gets boring, take up **bike polo** (also known as bicycle polo and cycle polo). This team sport is based on the traditional game of polo, in which people on horseback try to score goals by hitting a ball with a long stick. Each team has four players, who are allowed to hit the ball only when the bike is parallel to the sidelines. All players must use their right hand when striking the ball—sorry lefties! The official field is grass that measures 100 yards by 60 yards, but any size or type of field will do.

Off to the Races

People take part in all kinds of races, from running to sailing to flying. But those are too ordinary for some athletes. Here are a few of the most entertaining and unusual races that make for some extraordinary athletic events.

An Uphill Battle

Most people are happy taking an elevator to the top of the Empire State Building. But some people would rather race up the stairs. These athletes take part in the **Empire State Building Run-Up**. Every year, a few hundred athletes run up the quarter mile of steps to the top of the building. The racers huff and puff their way up the 1,576 stairs, often taking two steps at a time. The fastest get to the top in about 10 minutes. The payoff is a great view.

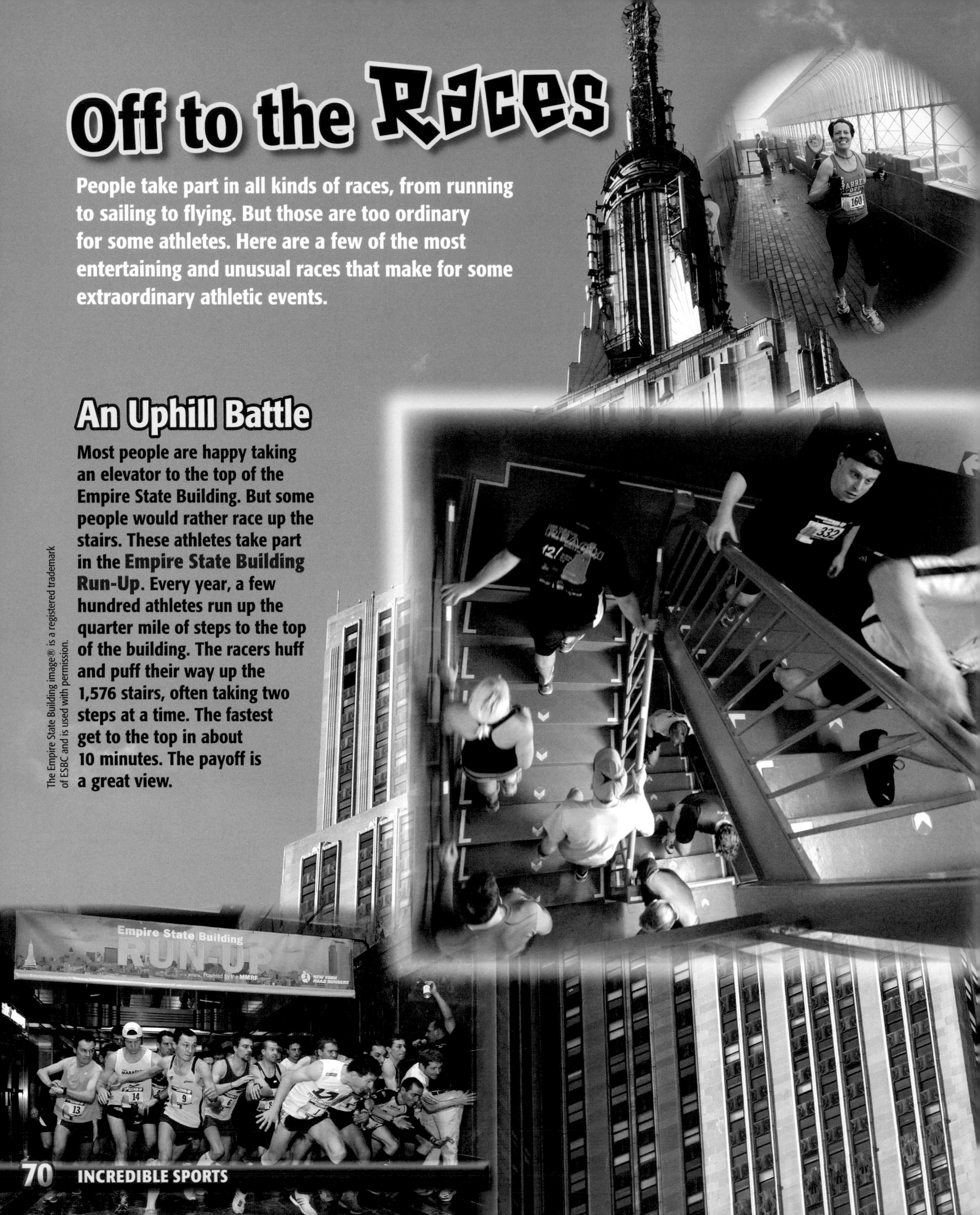

Bogged Down

A bog is a wetland filled with dead plant material. You wouldn't want to fall into one, let alone swim in it. Yet that's what about 200 people do every year outside a small town in Wales. It's the home of the World Bog Snorkeling Championships. The brave competitors put on snorkels and flippers and swim 60 yards and back through smelly, thick bog water. Bog racing takes place wherever there are bogs and people who like to swim in them.

BTW

In bog snorkeling, racers can only use their flippers to swim through the muck—using your arms to swim isn't allowed!

Cutting It Close

Try to imagine the Indianapolis 500 held with lawnmowers instead of race cars. That's what you'll see at the Twelve Mile 500 Riding Lawnmower Race. Held each July Fourth in Twelve Mile, Indiana, the 60-lap, 15-mile race is the granddaddy of all U.S. lawnmower races. Thirty-three riders soup up their engines—some of the lawnmowers hit speeds of 35 miles per hour. When the race is over, the machines go back to cutting grass.

Sports Bloopers...

Anyone can make a mistake—including sports stars. Some bloopers made by athletes are big news because they were the reason their teams lost. And sometimes sports screwups are just plain funny.

March Badness

The 1993 NCAA Men's Basketball Championship between Michigan and North Carolina had a blunderful ending. With 19 seconds to go, **Chris Webber** (wearing yellow in the photo) rebounded a Carolina miss. Michigan was trailing by two points as Webber dribbled down the court. As he crossed midcourt, he stopped dribbling and was immediately surrounded by Carolina players trying to steal the ball. In a panic, Webber called time out with 11 seconds left. Problem was, Michigan was out of time outs. By calling for one, Webber had committed a technical foul. Carolina made two free throws, and went on to win the championship 77–71.

For the Record

UCLA holds the record for the most NCAA men's Division 1 basketball championships, a total of 11. In second place is the University of Kentucky, with 7 titles. Third place is a tie between the University of North Carolina and Indiana University: Both have won 5 championships.

Through the Legs

Bill Buckner was a great baseball player who is remembered for one bad play. It took place during Game 6 of the 1986 World Series between the Boston Red Sox and the New York Mets. Up three games to two, the Sox needed one more game to win the Series. In the bottom of the 10th inning, the score was tied, with a man on third. The Mets' Mookie Wilson hit a slow ground ball to first. First baseman Buckner bent down to catch it, but the ball dribbled through his legs, as the winning run scored. The Mets won the game and the stunned Sox lost the next game—and the World Series.

Snow Fall

In the 2006 Winter Olympics held in Turin, Italy, **Lindsey Jacobellis** lost gold by making a goof. On the last run in the snowboard cross event, Jacobellis had a big lead on her nearest opponent. Close to the end of the run, she made her next-to-last jump. She added some unnecessary flair to the jump by grabbing her board in midair. Jacobellis's show-off move made her land on the side of her board and fall. Her competitor blew past her to win the gold. Jacobellis got silver.

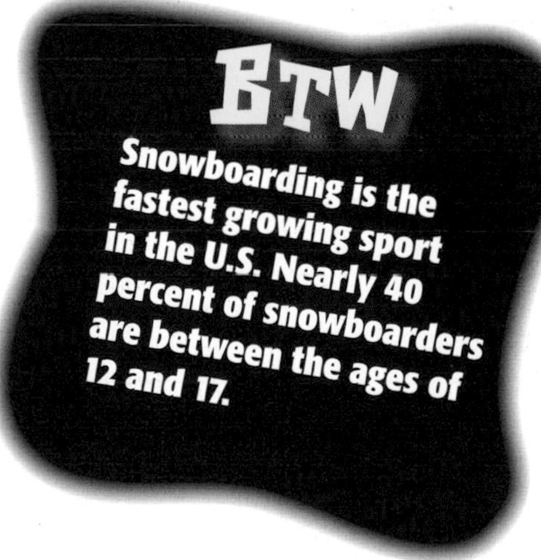

BTW
Snowboarding is the fastest growing sport in the U.S. Nearly 40 percent of snowboarders are between the ages of 12 and 17.

...and Blunders

Not all sports blunders are made by athletes. Some are made by fans and officials. When they change the outcome of the game, they become sports-blunders legends.

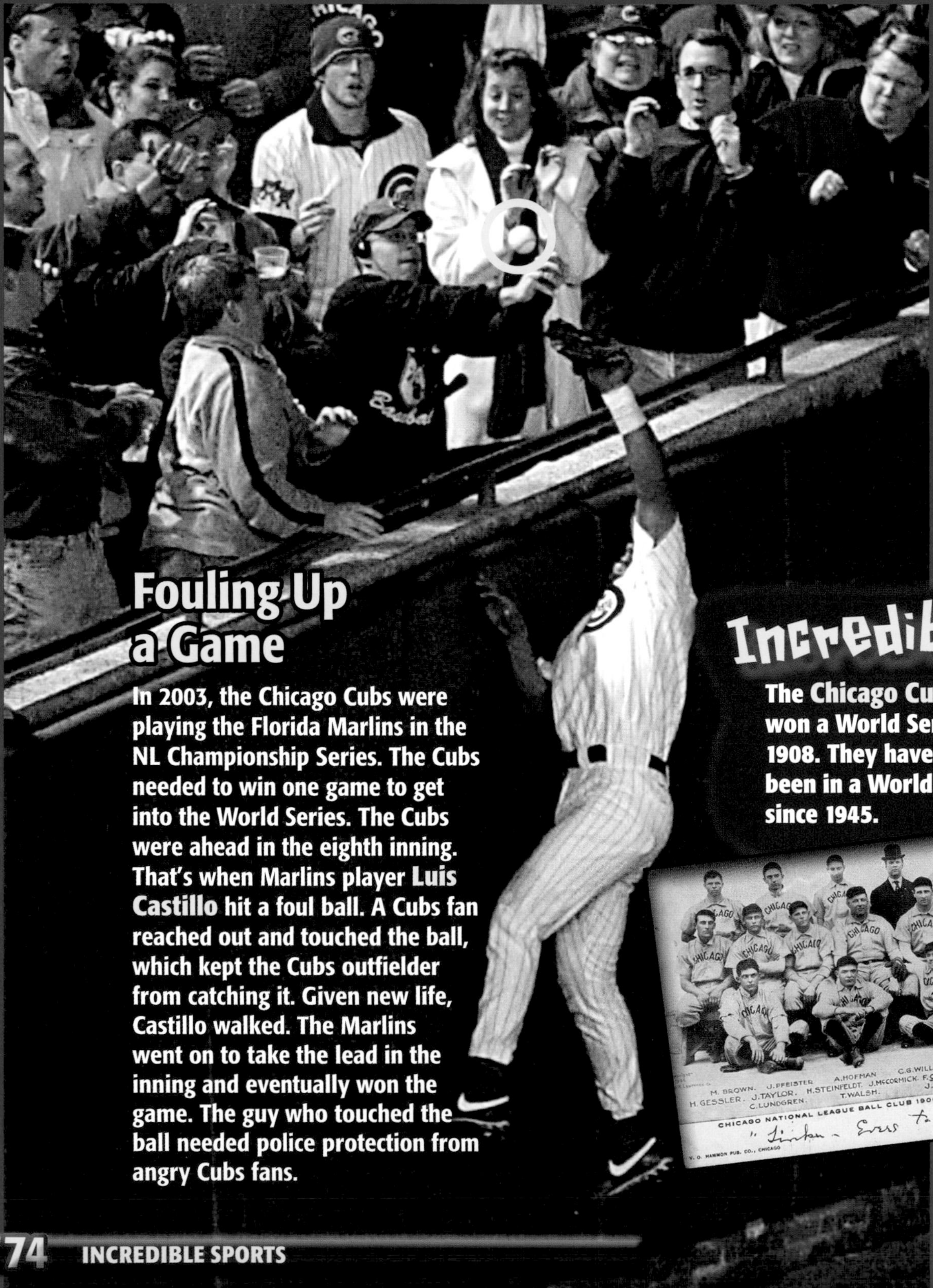

Fouling Up a Game

In 2003, the Chicago Cubs were playing the Florida Marlins in the NL Championship Series. The Cubs needed to win one game to get into the World Series. The Cubs were ahead in the eighth inning. That's when Marlins player **Luis Castillo** hit a foul ball. A Cubs fan reached out and touched the ball, which kept the Cubs outfielder from catching it. Given new life, Castillo walked. The Marlins went on to take the lead in the inning and eventually won the game. The guy who touched the ball needed police protection from angry Cubs fans.

Incredible!

The Chicago Cubs last won a World Series in 1908. They have not been in a World Series since 1945.

Not-So-Perfect Call

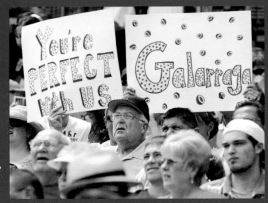

Detroit Tigers pitcher Armando Galarraga was perfect—but the umpire's call wasn't. In the ninth inning against the Cleveland Indians, Galarraga needed to get one more out to pitch a perfect game—meaning no players had reached base against him. The next player hit a grounder that was fielded by the first baseman. He threw the ball to Galarraga—who was covering first base—for the final out. But the umpire called the runner safe. Replays showed that the runner was clearly out. It didn't matter—Galarraga lost the perfect game and a no-hitter as well. The umpire later apologized to Galarraga.

For the Record

Only 20 pitchers have pitched perfect games in Major League Baseball history. The last to do it was Roy Halladay against the Florida Marlins in 2010. That same year, Halladay pitched a no-hitter in a playoff game against the Cincinnati Reds. It was only the second no-hitter pitched in a playoff game.

Pros and Pets

Pro athletes aren't just focused on the sports they play. Some players devote a lot of their time to their favorite pets—and often the pets they keep are pretty unusual. From creepy crawlers to furry critters, these best friends really score with the sports stars.

Cowboy Pirate

Ross Ohlendorf would never say, "Don't have a cow!" Ohlendorf is a pitcher for the Pittsburgh Pirates. But back home in Lockhart, Texas, he raises cows. Ohlendorf and his family run a ranch that is home to about 300 head of cattle. The cows are a type called longhorn, and they are bred and sold to other farms. But the cows have been with the family so long, they're more like pets. "We still have one of the first three that we bought," says Ohlendorf. "We've had her for 15 years. Her name is Marina." During the off-season, Ohlendorf names the calves, helps feed them, and puts pictures of the cows on the farm's website. Luckily, there is one job he gets to avoid: "I don't have to clean up after them."

BTW

Some of the names **Ohlendorf** has given to his cows are Cindy Crawford, Yahtzee, and Kickapoo.

Animal House

Ernie Sims would love to open a zoo one day. Actually, his house looks a bit like a zoo—it's packed with pets. The linebacker for the Philadelphia Eagles has dozens of reptiles, including two albino Burmese pythons, iguanas, bearded lizards, and alligators. He's not finished stocking his own little zoo with animals: "If I go into a pet store, I have to get something."

Horsing Around

Patrick Deneen is a freestyle skier who lives on a farm in Cle Elum, Washington. There, he and his family have four border collie dogs, a donkey named Mr. Don Key, and two miniature donkeys named Carlos and Shawnie. When Deneen isn't training or competing, he loves spending time with the animals. "When I'm home, I try to ride my horse a couple hours a day," he says. "It's a cool feeling."

BTW

Among **Deneen's freestyle skiing** honors are an International Ski Federation Rookie of the Year award in 2008 and gold medals at the World Ski Championships in 2009 and at the U.S. National Championships in 2011.

Extreme Snowmobiling

The 2011 Winter X Games were held at Buttermilk Mountain, in Aspen, Colorado. Competitors there showed off their skills in skiing, snowboarding, and snowmobiling events. In competitions like these, athletes perform jumps and tricks at full speed over snow. Extreme snowmobilers have to perform the same kind of stunts—but on 500-pound machines!

Incredible!

The longest snowmobile race in the world is Alaska's Tesoro Iron Dog. It covers 2,000 miles.

Snow Much Fun

One of the oldest and most popular snowmobiling events is snocross. The event was inspired by motocross, a race held on motorcycles on a dirt track. In snocross, up to 12 riders race on a track that has sharp, banked corners, tight turns, steep jumps, and obstacles. The short course is made as difficult to get around as possible. Even so, riders go up to 60 miles per hour and make jumps as high as 30 feet. Before touching down, athletes can travel as much as 130 feet in the air. Not surprisingly, racers must wear goggles, helmets, and other protective gear.

Big Air

In freestyle snowmobiling, riders test their skills and nerve by zooming up a steep ramp at full speed and flying through the air. Athletes can travel from 65 feet to more than 100 feet before they land on the snow. While in midair, they must perform tricks, such as holding onto the seat with one hand, dangling from an upside down machine, or standing on the seat.

Chapter 4
Incredible Food

Food is fuel. We eat to keep our bodies going and to stay healthy. Food also tastes good (Well, many foods taste good!), so we eat because it's enjoyable. But some people do more with food than just eat it. Some artists turn food into the most amazing objects. These tasty-looking creations can make your mouth water and tickle your funny bone at the same time. Even though the artworks aren't edible, they are a feast for the eyes.

In This Chapter

- Bread Art
- Fish Egg Monsters
- The Great Wall of... Chocolate!

And Much More!

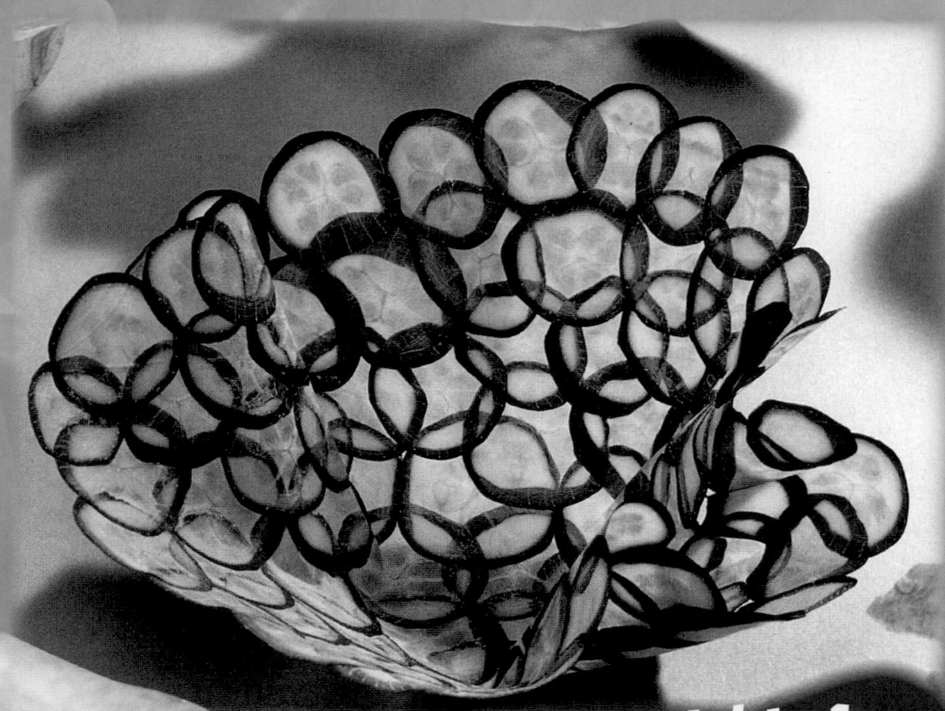

Incredible!

Food lovers will be bowled over by the bowls that Margaret Dorfman makes: They are made out of fruits and vegetables. She slices them thin, shapes them by hand, and covers them with a clear finish. Do you recognize the vegetable this one is made from? (The answer is upside down.)

Answer: zucchini

Incredible!

A nacho hat can keep your head warm or fill your belly. It is made from baked tortilla dough, and it even has an opening at the top to put in salsa. And any broken chips will land on the brim. Olé!

Blast from the Past

Chocolate first came to China in the 1700s. A European brought the emperor of China 150 bars of chocolate to be used as medicine. It was to be eaten with sugar and hot water. Well, it certainly couldn't hurt!

Chocolate Dreams

Willy Wonka would have loved this place. The World Chocolate Dream Park, located in Beijing, the capital of China, is a sweet place to hang out. In this mouth-watering theme park, visitors can see chocolates of every shape and size, from huge sculptures to candies they can eat. Eighty tons of Belgian chocolate were used to build the park. The exhibits are inside glass panels and are air conditioned to keep all that chocolate from melting.

High-Calorie Car

The park displays U.S. dollar bills, a chess set, a handbag, and sneakers—all made from chocolate. One of the coolest objects is a full-size car, a BMW, made of chocolate. Does it run on chocolate syrup?

Sweet Soldiers

The famous terra cotta warriors (see page 90) are made of chocolate-colored clay. These terra cotta soldiers are made of chocolate-colored chocolate. The mini army of 560 soldiers, each about 10 inches high, stands at attention on a field of chocolate flakes.

Chocolate Cave

The Dunhuang Mogao Grottoes in Northwest China are famous for containing 2,000 statues of the Buddha, the founding figure of a religion called Buddhism. On display is a chocolate version showing about 100 Buddhist sculptures, each about 8.5 inches tall.

A Really Great Wall

The Great Wall of China is nearly 4,000 miles long and 30 feet high. The Great Chocolate Wall is only about 36 feet long and four feet high, but it may be more impressive—it's definitely tastier. The wall was built from solid dark chocolate bricks stuck together with white chocolate. One end of the wall is crumbled just like the real version.

Incredible!

If you ate about 3½ ounces of the Great Chocolate Wall every day, it would take 180 years to finish it. It is made of seven tons of chocolate and took six months to complete.

It Looks Good Enough to Eat

Don't play with your food. That advice may be good for most people, but it's not for some artists and designers. They are very playful with food, and have used it to create all sorts of incredible objects. The food art is meant to make people smile and stretch their imaginations—but it's not meant to be eaten!

Quite A-Peeling

This apple won't keep a doctor away. But could it help you get an A on a geography test? The artist, **Kevin Van Aelst**, carved a delicious apple into a globe of the world and took the picture before it turned brown. Van Aelst likes to take ordinary objects and turn them into something completely different.

Slice of Life

Any way you slice it, **Catherine McEver** creates amazing art. She sews thread through slices of white bread to make scenes of nature and copies of famous paintings, such as Vincent Van Gogh's *Starry Night* (pictured below). How does she sew the bread? Very carefully. McEver says that some of her bread art has stayed fresh for as long as four years.

Fishy Art

The artist **Vic Muniz** uses peanut butter, chocolate, pasta, and even caviar—eggs from a species of fish called sturgeon—in his art work. For this portrait of *Frankenstein*, part of a series of classic horror movie monsters made out of caviar, he used almost 20 ounces of the expensive fish eggs. Then he took a photo of it. Once photographed, the actual caviar portrait was discarded.

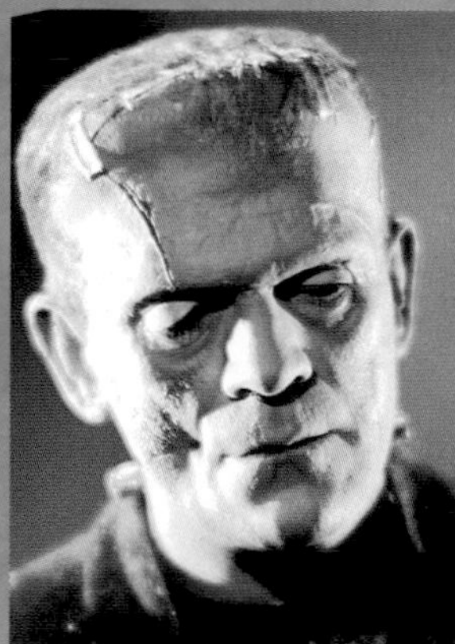

Boris Karloff played the monster in the 1931 horror film *Frankenstein*. It is considered one of the scariest movies ever made.

BTW

Considered by some food lovers to be a tasty treat, caviar can be very costly. The black caviar used by Muniz in his portraits costs more than 100 dollars an ounce.

Chapter 5 Incredible Arts

Leonardo da Vinci created great pictures—but he never made a portrait out of snack food. Michelangelo carved great sculptures. But he never used crayons instead of marble. Today's artists create artworks out of just about any material, no matter how unusual—whether it's cassette tape, screws, or cereal.

In This Chapter

- An Army of Life-Size Clay Soldiers
- Miniature *Zoo*diac
- A Presidential Portrait Made of Cereal

And Much More!

Incredible!

To make art from screws, Andrew Myers first draws a portrait on a board. Then he figures out where the screws should go over the drawing and how deep each should be. This is a self-portrait.

Incredible!

Artist Diem Chau doesn't use crayons to draw pictures. Instead, Chau carves the Crayolas into colorful, skinny sculptures of people, animals, and objects. There is a set showing the symbols of 10 different world currencies (right). Can you pick out the symbol of the U.S. cent? One of Chau's most amazing feats was creating the 12 animals of the Chinese Zodiac (left). Each animal is a symbol of a year, and anyone born during that year supposedly has the animal's traits. Can you identify the 12 animals? (The answers are upside down below.)

Blast from the Past

China's terra cotta army is amazing! The life-size clay soldiers were discovered in 1974, and they include 8,000 soldiers, 130 chariots, and more than 500 horses.

Answers: The U.S. cent sign is the brown crayon. The animals of the Chinese Zodiac are, from left to right: monkey, pig, goat, snake, rat, rooster, dragon, horse, dog, rabbit, tiger, and ox.

Sand-Sational Sculptures

Most castles are made of brick or stone and are built to stand for hundreds of years. A sand castle lasts until the tide comes in and washes it away. Although they don't last for centuries, sand castles and sand sculptures can be pretty impressive. You don't have to live near an ocean to create a sand sculpture. You can build one anywhere there is sand, even in a sand box.

Beauty and the Beach

Copacabana beach is a long, wide stretch of sand on the edge of Rio de Janeiro, a city in Brazil. People swim, sunbathe, and play volleyball and other games. Most fun of all, they build sand sculptures, like this amazing castle.

Just Plane Amazing!

Every year, some of the best sand sculptors in Japan and elsewhere come to the Fukiage Sand Sculpture Festival in Kagoshima, Japan. Tons of sand are dumped in the festival area for the artists to make their sand magic. This sculpture of **Charles Lindbergh and his airplane** was carved by four people. In 1927, Lindbergh became the first person to fly non-stop solo across the Atlantic Ocean. The flight took 33½ hours.

Make Your Own Sand Sculpture

Here are some tips on becoming a master sand sculptor.

- Don't add sand to your sculpture or castle. That will cause it to crumble. Instead, carve away sand, working from top to bottom.
- Make sure the sand is damp. Dry sand won't hold up.
- To keep your sculpture moist, use a spray mister filled with seawater or fresh water mixed with salt. When it dries, the salt crystals form a crust over the sculpture, keeping it firm.
- Don't use your hands to remove loose sand. Instead, use a straw to blow it away.
- Use any objects you can find to carve sand: spoons, cookie cutters, even shells. You can also decorate a sculpture with found objects.

An All-Sand Cast

The International Sand Sculpture Festival, held near the village of Pera, in Portugal, is sand-tastic. Inspired by a Hollywood theme, 60 artists created sandy versions of King Kong, the Simpsons, the dinosaurs in *Jurassic Park*, Darth Vader, and this incredible version of the ***Chronicles of Narnia***. The sculpture features the Lion Aslan, the children, and the wardrobe.

For the Record

The tallest sand sculpture on record was created in China by a group of 30 artists. It took 75 days to complete the nearly 74-foot-tall masterpiece.

Feats of Clay

In 1974, farmers digging a well in China discovered three pits filled with more than 7,000 life-size clay sculptures of soldiers, horses, and chariots. They were made of a type of clay called terra cotta (terr-ah *cot*-ah). The figures, placed near the tomb of the first Emperor of China, in 210 B.C., stand at attention. And they've caught the attention of the world: Thousands of people visit the city of Xian in order to see this incredible army.

The life-size warriors range in height from 5 feet 8 inches to 6 feet 6 inches. The higher a soldier's rank, the taller he is. The smallest figures are foot soldiers. Soldiers who rode in chariots are taller. Generals and other officers are tallest.

Incredible!

Qin Shihuangdi, the first Emperor of China, did things in a big way. In addition to the clay army, he ordered a 20-square-mile tomb to be built. It took 700,000 workers 36 years to create this underground city, which he supposedly filled with models of palaces, towers, and a river of mercury. It was protected by crossbows that triggered automatically to shoot any intruder. It will take many years to dig up the site.

The lower bodies of the soldiers are solid clay, and the upper parts are hollow. That made it easier for the statues to stand upright. Heads, caps, shoes, and other parts were made in molds, then attached with strips of wet clay.

The face of each soldier was carved individually, so they all look different. Some soldiers have beards or mustaches, some have caps, and there are many types of hairstyles. All these details make the soldiers look more lifelike.

BTW

To preserve the sculptures, they are sprayed with a special clear liquid that bonds to the clay.

Real weapons, including bows and arrows, spears, and swords, were also found in the pits. Some of the weapons have been stolen by thieves, who set fire to the wooden roof that covered the clay army. When the roof collapsed, the soldiers were buried—and remained so for more than 2,000 years.

Face It!

A portrait shows the likeness of a person. Artists often paint portraits with oils or draw them with pencil or pen. But just about any type of material—from snack food to broken CDs and pasta—has been used to create a picture of a person.

Snack Art

This portrait of President Barack Obama is titled *Breakfast of Champions*. Artists Hank Willis Thomas and Ryan Alexiev made it out of thousands of bits of breakfast cereal.

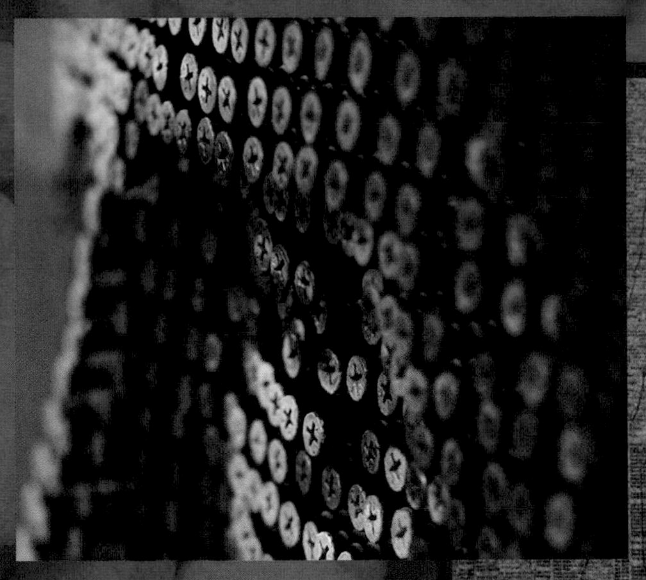

Screwy Picture

Artist **Andrew Myers** created this **self-portrait** out of screws. He started by drilling holes into wood. He then drilled in the screws and painted the head of each one. Myers uses between 8,000 and 10,000 screws for a portrait, and it takes up to six months to finish.

King of Pop Art

This portrait of **Michael Jackson** is made out of used cassette tape that flows out of an old cassette. The artist, **Erika Iris Simmons**, doesn't like to see out-of-date objects go to waste. Reusing things is good for the environment—and for artists.

Blast from the Past

Before there were CDs and MP3s, most people popped a cassette tape into a tape recorder to hear music. This plastic tape was a popular way to listen to recorded music between the 1970s and the 1990s.

Chapter 6 Incredible Earth

The Earth seems to be a solid and stable ball, but it is alive and active. The crust of the Earth constantly moves, forming mountains and causing earthquakes. Wind and water forever rearrange the face of the planet. Earth is ever-changing and full of exciting–and sometimes fierce–surprises.

In This Chapter

- Deadly Waves
- The Earth at Night from Space
- Underground Wonders
- The Deepest Lake in the World

And Much More!

Incredible!

This photo taken from the International Space Station shows Tokyo, the capital of Japan, and nearby areas.

BTW

Rock on! This spectacular sandstone arch, called Delicate Arch, was carved by wind and rain over millions of years. It's one of many amazing rock formations—including 2,000 sandstone arches—found in Arches National Park, in Utah. This 52-foot-high arch is the most famous landmark in Utah: It appears on state license plates and on a 1996 postage stamp.

Killer Waves

A tsunami (soo-*nah*-mee) is one of the fiercest forces of nature. Tsunami is a Japanese word that means "harbor wave." These waves start in the ocean and when they hit land, they may sweep away everything in their path, including houses, boats, trains, and cars. Small tsunamis happen about once a year somewhere in the world. Really big ones hit less often, but when they do, they can cause great destruction.

The Japanese Tsunami

In 2011, a massive earthquake struck in the Pacific Ocean, 80 miles off the coast of Japan. The quake caused a tsunami with waves as high as a three-story building. The tsunami hit the east coast of Japan, and as it roared inland, it swept away entire cities. The tsunami was so powerful that it crossed the Pacific Ocean and reached California.

BTW

The quake hit where the North American and Pacific plates meet. It was caused by a sudden shift of the Pacific plate under the North American plate.

How a Tsunami Forms

A tsunami is produced by earthquakes, underwater landslides, exploding volcanoes, and even big meteorites that crash into the ocean. Undersea quakes happen when sections of the Earth's crust, called plates, collide. The collision moves huge amounts of water, causing waves to form. The long ocean waves gather strength and height, and spill onto land. The tsunami that struck Japan in 2011 was set off by an undersea earthquake.

1. The Collision

The upward shift of the North American plate releases a lot of energy. Vast volumes of water are displaced, causing a tsunami.

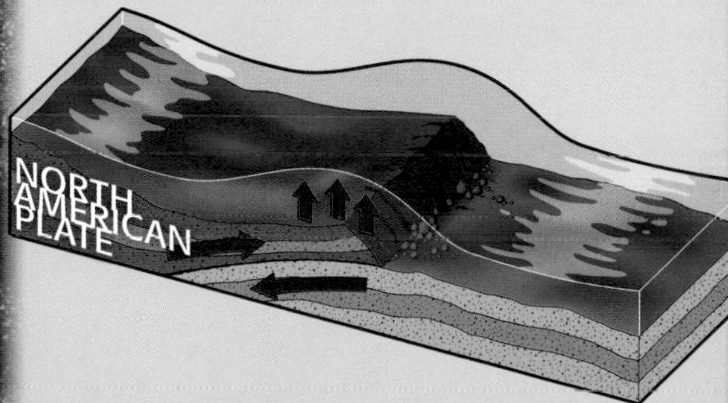

2. The Tsunami

In the sea, the waves start out long and low. The tsunami gains power and height as it speeds toward land.

Incredible!

The quake that triggered the Japanese tsunami was so strong that it moved Japan 13 feet closer to the U.S. and shifted the Earth's axis slightly.

Extreme Geography

Earth is covered by a jumble of geographical features. There are soaring mountains, lush forests, dry deserts, long rivers, deep oceans, and endless other landforms and bodies of water. Some of these features stand out more than others. Here are some of the biggest, tallest, longest, and other kinds of "-est."

Biggest Island

The biggest island in the world, **Greenland** is about 20 times larger than the country that it belongs to: Denmark. Greenland is 839,999 square miles, making it larger than all but 33 countries. Much of Greenland is covered by ice. That's not surprising since the island is only 450 miles from the North Pole.

BTW

About 81 percent of Greenland is covered by ice.

Tallest Mountain

Mauna Kea is 13,796 feet tall measured from the surface of the Pacific Ocean. But measured from the ocean floor, this volcano on the island of Hawaii is the tallest mountain in the world. From base to peak, Mauna Kea is more than six miles tall–half a mile taller than Mount Everest, the tallest mountain measured from sea level. The height of Mauna Kea and the clear air around it are reasons it's the home of the world's largest, most powerful telescope–the **Keck telescope**.

Lowest Point

The **Dead Sea**, which borders Jordan, Israel, and the West Bank, is the lowest point on the surface of the Earth. The surface of the lake is 1,349 feet below sea level. The Dead Sea is about eight times saltier than the ocean, so swimmers enjoy floating on it. But don't take a dip if you have a cut–the salty water stings!

Deepest (and oldest) Lake

Located in a region of Russia called Siberia, **Lake Baikal** is the oldest (25 million years) and the deepest lake (more than a mile down) in the world. It contains 20 percent of all the liquid freshwater in the world. Lake Baikal teems with life, containing more than 1,800 species of animals and plants.

The World at Night

This photo of Earth at night was taken from a satellite in orbit, and it shows permanent lights on the planet's surface. The brightest dots are the biggest cities. Connecting some dots are thin lines that show roads, railroad tracks, and even large rivers. Some regions are completely black, such as the polar regions, deserts, forests, and mountains. More urban areas are lit up like a Christmas tree. Can you find where you live?

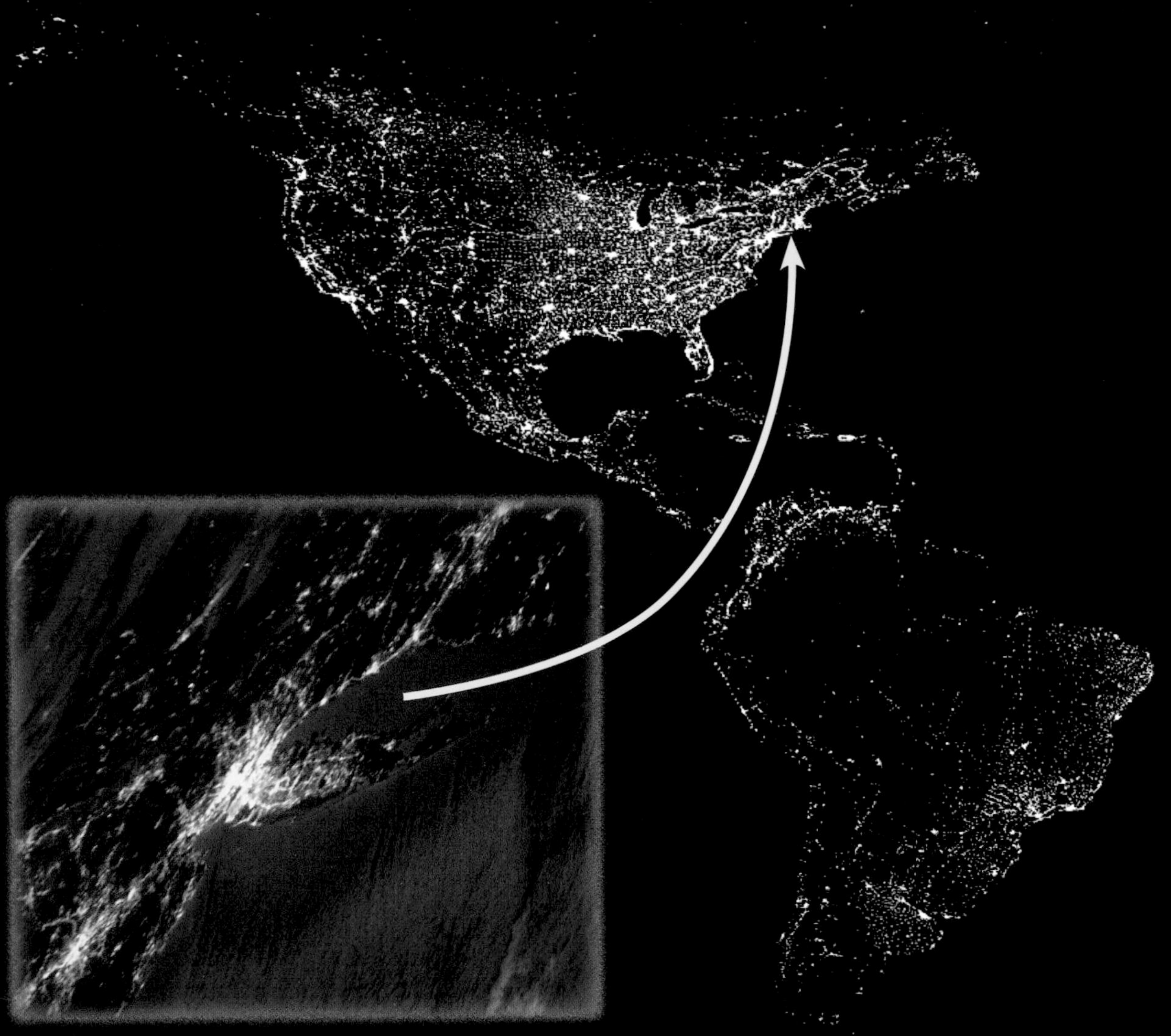

This photo, taken from the International Space Station, shows the East Coast of the U.S. at night. The brightest lights, in the center, are from New York City. South of New York is Philadelphia, and the lit up areas north of New York are cities in Connecticut.

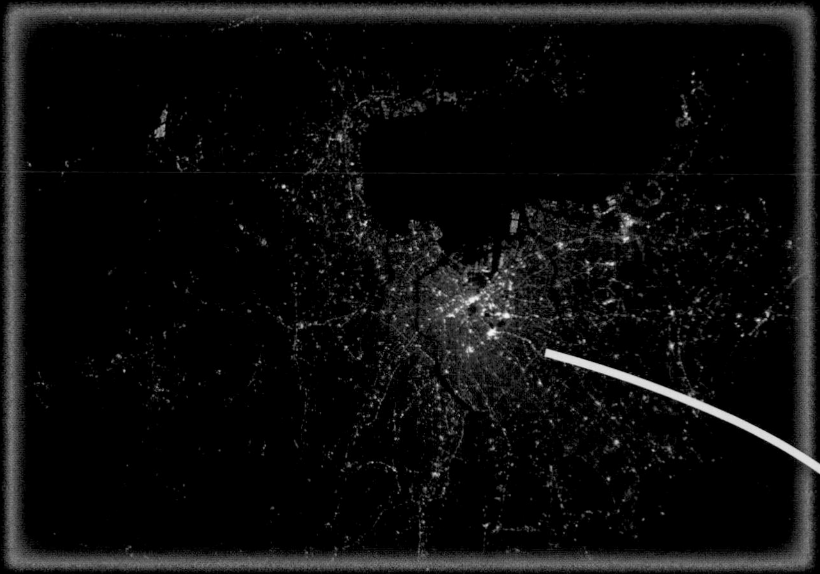

This photo, also taken from the International Space Station, shows Tokyo, the capital of Japan, and the area around the city.

BTW

The image of the entire Earth was put together from data gathered over nine months by NASA satellites orbiting at a height of about 500 miles. The satellites were originally used by the U.S. Air Force to view clouds by moonlight and help pilots fly at night. Now the satellites are used to study Earth's environment, especially to see how urban areas are expanding.

What do diamonds, sapphires, rubies, and emeralds have in common? They are all gemstones. A gemstone is a rare, beautiful, and hard mineral that's usually used to make jewelry. When a gemstone is cut and polished, it's called a gem. What makes a gem valuable? Its color and the way light makes it sparkle are two ways people judge a gem. And its size can be important: Often, the bigger a stone, the more expensive it is.

A Diamond in the Rough

In 1905, miners in South Africa found what they thought was a piece of broken glass. It turned out to be a diamond gemstone that weighed 1.5 pounds and was nearly four inches long. It was the biggest uncut diamond ever found, at 3,100 carats. (A carat is how gems are measured. Ten carats are equal to one-tenth of an ounce.) Eventually, the gemstone was cut into several diamonds. The largest of them, called the **Star of Africa**, weighs 530.20 carats. It is part of the British Crown Jewels that are kept in the Tower of London.

Incredible!

The largest diamond in the galaxy is 10 billion trillion trillion carats and is 2,500 miles across. To get to it, you have to travel about 300 trillion miles. The cosmic-size gem is actually the core of a burned-out star called a white dwarf. When the star died, its center turned into a carbon crystal, otherwise known as a diamond.

Looking Blue

The **Hope Diamond** isn't the biggest diamond in the world—it's the size of a walnut—but it might be the most famous. It's part of the gem collection of the Smithsonian Institution, in Washington, D.C. Tens of thousands of visitors pass it every day, making it one of the most popular museum objects in the world. The Hope Diamond is dark blue, which makes it very rare. Its history is also special. The diamond was owned by French and English kings. And it comes with a curse: Supposedly anyone who wears it will have bad luck.

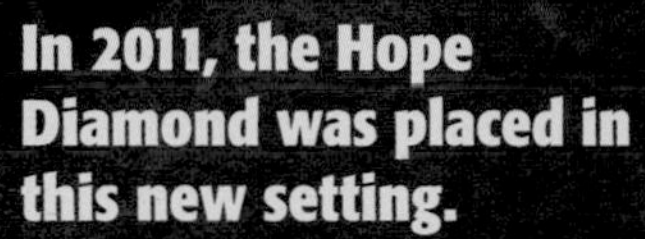

In 2011, the Hope Diamond was placed in this new setting.

BTW

Moon rocks aren't gems, but they are almost as valuable. A moon rock the size of a raisin is worth about $5 million. But having one could send you to jail: It's against the law for a private citizen to have a moon rock unless it was bought from someone who was given the rock by NASA or the U.S. government.

That's Some Pearl

A pearl forms inside the shell of a mollusk, such as an oyster or a clam. Pearls are called organic gems because they come from living things. They are usually no bigger than small grapes. But the **Pearl of Lao Tzu** is the mother of all pearls. The humongous pearl weighs about 14 pounds and is worth about $60 million.

Peak Experiences

Climbing the Seven Summits is a tall order. The Seven Summits is the name for the tallest peak on each of the seven continents: Africa, Antarctica, Asia, Australia, Europe, North America, and South America. For mountaineers, reaching the tops of all seven is a high point in their climbing experience.

1

The Tallest of All

Mount Everest is the highest peak in Asia—and the world. It is 29,035 feet high, and at its summit the wind can reach 125 miles per hour, the temperatures can drop as low as -100°F, and the air is thin and hard to breathe. Its height and dangers make it the ultimate goal for climbers.

7

6

5

Alaska's Pride

North America's tallest peak, **Mount McKinley**, is in Alaska. Native peoples call the 20,320-foot mountain Denali, which means "The High One." Many people have reached its often frigid summit, but many others have died in the attempt.

7

6

Peak of Perfection

The highest peak in South America—or anywhere else outside of Asia—is the 22,831-foot **Mount Aconcagua**. Part of the mighty Andes mountain chain, the massive peak is located in Argentina. Cold, dry air, high winds, and the danger of falling rocks and avalanches make this mountain a challenge to climb.

High and Mighty

Mount Elbrus, in Russia, is the highest peak in Europe. More than 70 glaciers, or rivers of ice, flow down from the top of the 18,510-foot mountain. During the brutal, windy winters, few climbers dare go for the summit. It took the extreme athlete in the photo two days to reach the peak and only one minute to glide down to the bottom. He was wearing a special suit that resembles a bird.

High Riser

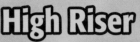

Mount Kilimanjaro, the highest mountain in Africa, is located in Tanzania. At 19,340 feet, it is the tallest peak that is not part of a mountain range. Mount Kilimanjaro can be dangerous to climb because of its cold temperatures.

On Top Down Under

The tallest mountain in Australia is **Mount Kosciuszko** (koz-kee-*uhs*-koh). Of the Seven Summits, the 7,310-foot mountain is the easiest to climb. About 100,000 people make the two-hour hike to its summit each year.

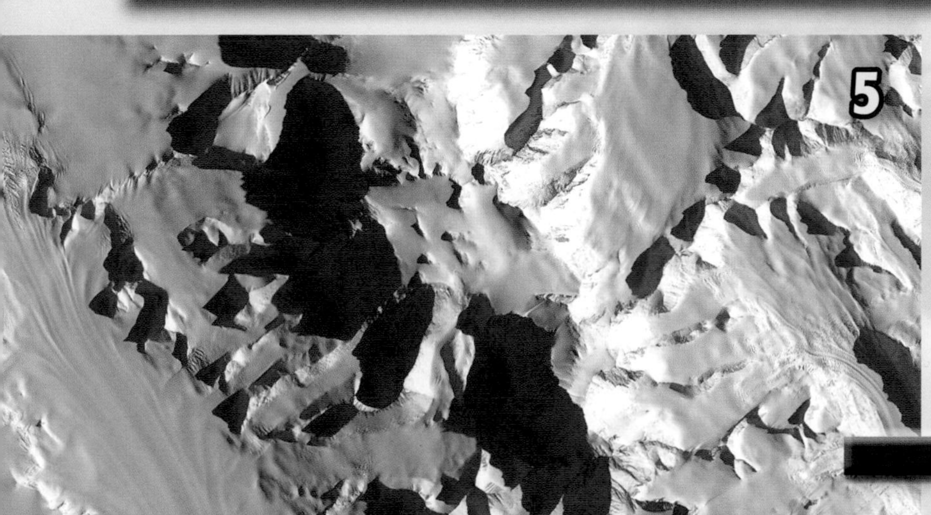

Frozen Heights

The **Vinson Massif** in Antarctica, seen here from space, might be the toughest of all mountains to climb. That's because climbers have to travel through frigid Antarctica to reach it. Only 700 people have ever tried to reach its 16,066-foot peak.

Nature Rocks!

A rock is a hard object. But over time, erosion can wear down even the hardest rocks. Flowing rivers, wind, seawater, and other types of weathering can, over hundreds, thousands, or even millions of years, turn rocks into just about any shape. Some rocks look as if humans carved them into familiar objects, such as mushrooms or a person's face. But it's nature that sculpted these incredible shapes.

Fake Fungus

This mushroom is too tough to eat. The cap of the 'shroom is made from sandstone that didn't erode as much as the softer "stem" below it. The **Mushroom Rock State Park**, in Kansas, not only has a rock mushroom, but many other oddly shaped rocks.

Blast from the Past

Wondrous ancient buildings and statues have been carved out of sandstone, including the sandstone city of **Petra**, in Jordan.

Face the Nation

There are many rock formations that look like human faces. Maybe the most famous is the **Old Man of the Mountain**, located in the White Mountains of New Hampshire. Rocks that stuck out from the mountain looked just like the side of a man's face. The profile was 40 feet tall and 25 feet wide. Unfortunately, the face collapsed in 2003. But it lives on, featured on the state quarter of New Hampshire.

NEW HAMPSHIRE 1788
LIVE FREE OR DIE
OLD MAN OF THE MOUNTAIN
2000
E PLURIBUS UNUM

A Gnome's Home?

Are these the homes of trolls, elves, and other creatures from a fairy tale? The pillars, columns, needles, and towers were carved by wind and water from volcanic rock. Known as the **Goreme Valley fairy chimneys**, they are a big tourist attraction in Turkey.

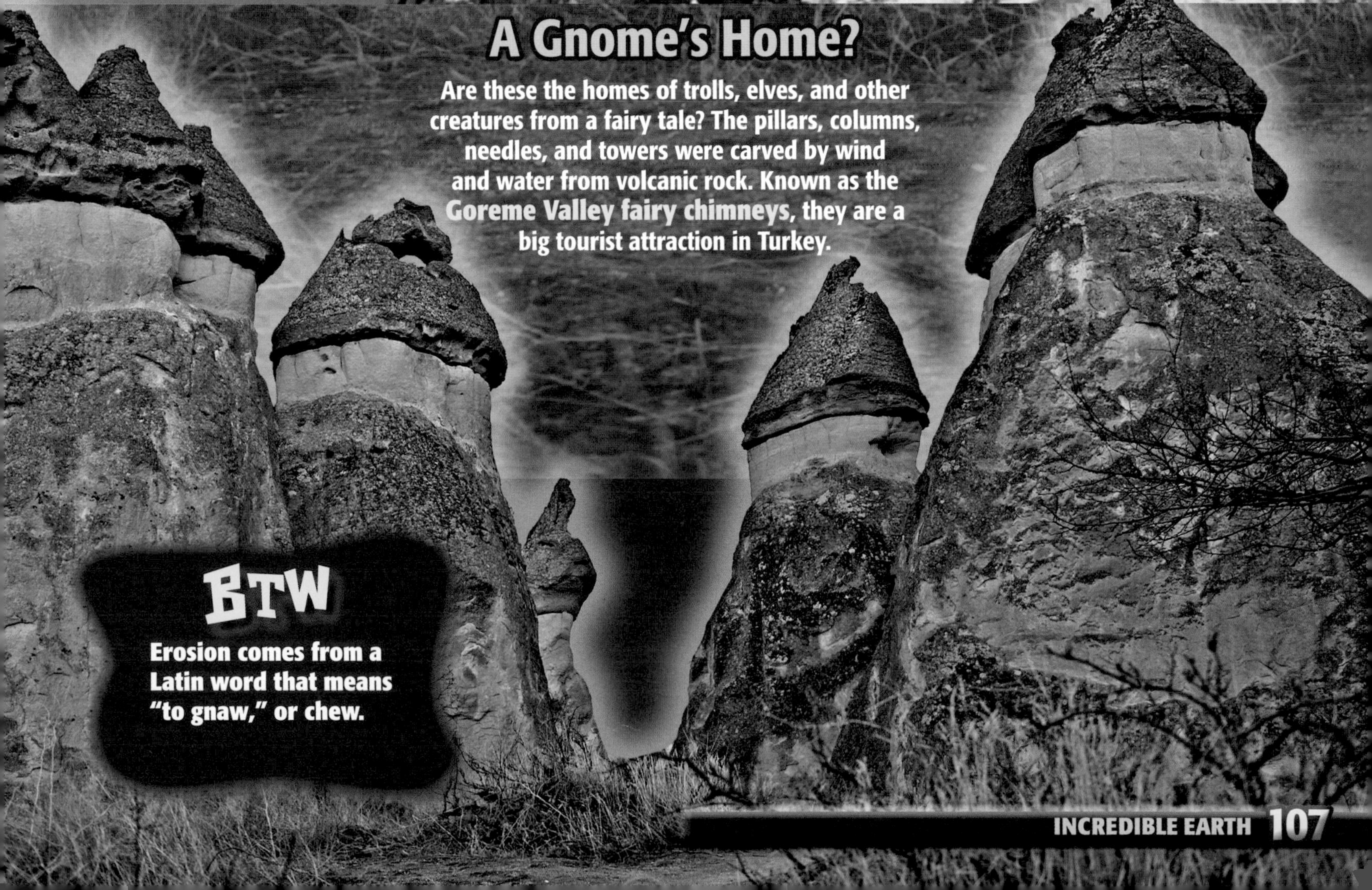

BTW

Erosion comes from a Latin word that means "to gnaw," or chew.

Underground Wonderlands

Caves and passageways deep below Earth's surface hold incredible treasures. They don't contain pirate gold, but something far more fantastic: spectacular underground scenery. Waterfalls of liquid and ice and columns of crystal are some of the wonders you can find below ground.

All Falls Down

Ruby Falls astonished the people who discovered it in 1928. And the underground waterfall still amazes visitors. Ruby Falls is located more than 1,000 feet below the surface. It's in a cave that's part of Lookout Mountain Caverns, in Chattanooga, Tennessee. An underground stream feeds the towering falls, which drop 145 feet into a pool of water that's pure enough to drink.

Incredible!

The Grotte Casteret, a limestone cave in Spain, has a frozen waterfall. The cave is so cold that water that flows down freezes almost instantly into giant icicles and columns of clear ice.

Out-of-Control Crystals

The largest natural crystals in the world are in the Cave of Crystals in Mexico. Some of the crystals are 36 feet long and weigh up to 55 tons. A combination of high temperatures and water with a high mineral content help make the crystals grow extra large. The cave was accidentally discovered by miners. Water was pumped out so the crystals could be studied, but the crystals will not continue to grow without the water. Scientists wonder if they should keep the water out of the cave so the crystals can be seen, or they should let the water seep back in so the crystals can grow but can't be studied. What do you think?

Chapter 7

Incredible Space

What's up? The answer is a universe full of unknown worlds and mysterious objects. Every day, telescopes on Earth and in orbit, as well as space probes whizzing around the solar system, are giving us incredible images and information about these heavenly bodies. Our quick trip through the cosmos is one thrilling ride.

In This Chapter

- When Galaxies Collide
- The Biggest Mountain in the Solar System
- Space Trash Circles Earth
- Sun-sational Flares
- High-Impact Craters

And Much More!

BTW

One of the world's largest craters is the Wolfe Creek Crater, in Australia. Formed about 300,000 years ago, the crater is more than a half-mile across. The meteorite that made it weighed about 110 million pounds. It made a hole as deep as a 40-story building, which has mostly been filled in by sand.

For the Record

The surface of Enceladus, a moon of Saturn, reflects almost 100 percent of the sunlight that hits it.

Incredible!

The sun is about 864,000 miles across. You could pack more than one million Earths inside it.

Cosmic Collisions

Earth has been hit by space rocks throughout its history. Some of those collisions were powerful enough to wipe out much of life on the planet. When stars and galaxies collide, an unbelievable amount of energy is released. This energy helps make the universe an ever-changing, ever-more incredible place.

Smashing Planets

Because the universe is a big place, stars don't often collide. But in certain areas of space, there are double stars—two stars that orbit around each other. Sometimes the stars get closer and closer to each other, until they collide. As the stars pull together, their gravity can bump nearby planets out of orbit. Scientists think that this would make the planets collide.

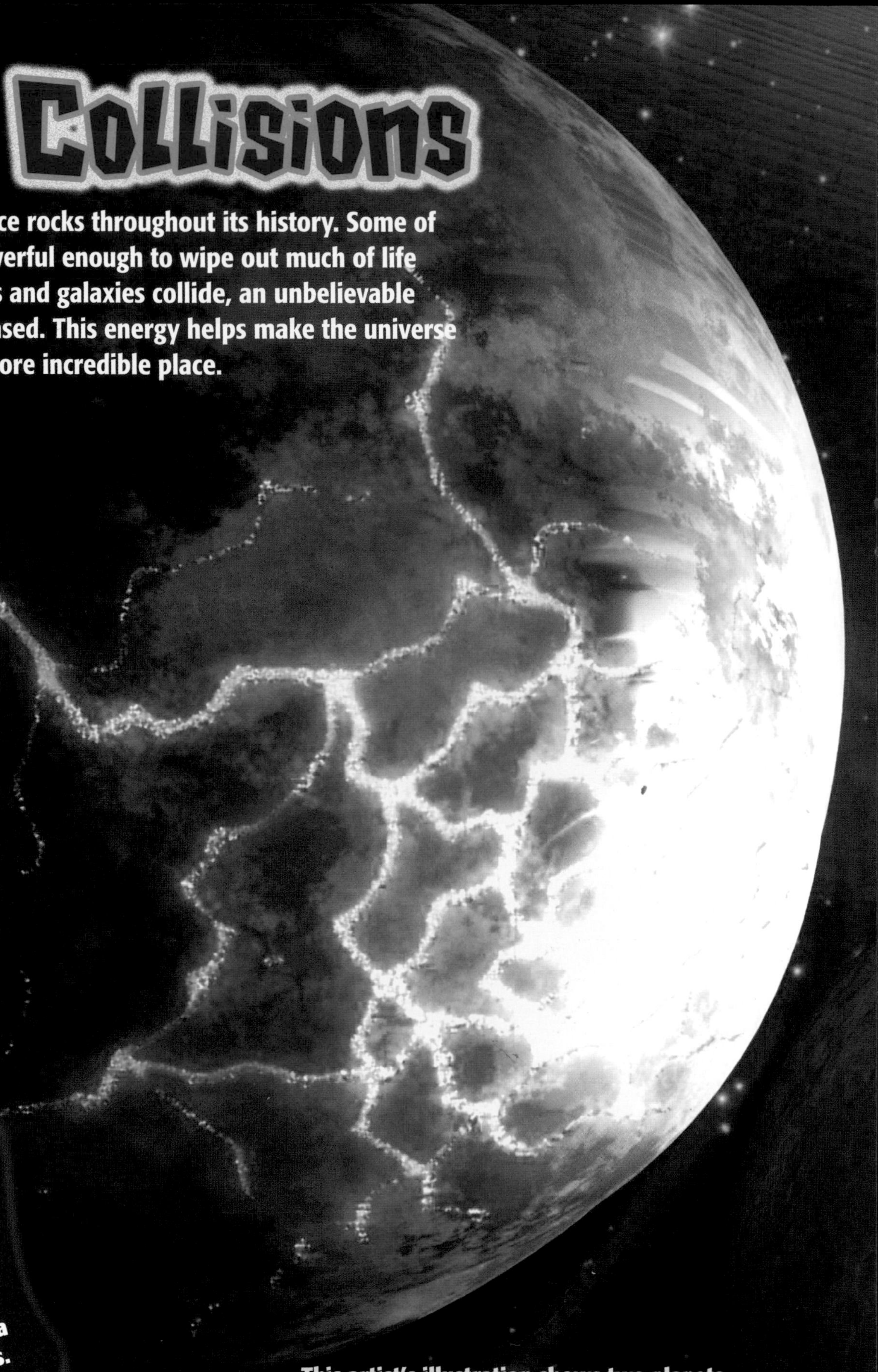

Incredible!

Scientists believe there are 100 billion to a trillion galaxies in the universe. Those galaxies contain about 300 sextillion stars. That's a 3 followed by 23 zeros.

This artist's illustration shows two planets that orbit double stars. The planets are about to hit, and the gravity of one planet is causing the other to crack apart.

Crash Course

A **galaxy** is a large group of stars, dust, and gas held together by gravity. There are often hundreds of billions of stars in a galaxy. As big as they are, galaxies move fast: The Milky Way, the galaxy our solar system is part of, travels at 1.3 million miles per hour. Not surprisingly, galaxies sometimes collide. This photo shows two spiral-shaped galaxies running into each other. Over the next few billion years, they will tear each other up until only one big galaxy remains.

BTW

Our galaxy, the Milky Way, is on a crash course with the nearby Andromeda galaxy. But don't worry: The collision won't happen for another three billion years. So, that's not an excuse to skip your homework!

The Solar System's Wonders

From water vapor geysers on a moon of Saturn shooting thousands of miles into space, to a mammoth Martian mountain, our solar system is full of mega-size wonders.

Eye on Io

Io (*eye*-oh) is only the third largest moon of Jupiter. But it has something the others don't: erupting volcanoes. In fact, Io has more active volcanoes than any other place in the solar system. About the size of Earth's moon, Io has a molten center that erupts through the surface. The gases shoot out through 80 volcanoes and 300 cracks in the surface. Where the volcanoes erupt, temperatures reach 2,240°F. Except for the sun, that's the hottest surface temperature in the solar system.

The small photo shows lava coming out of a volcano erupting on Io.

The Great Geysers of Enceladus

Enceladus (en-*sell*-ah-duss) is a moon of Saturn. It is covered by white ice that scientists think may hide an ocean of liquid water. The evidence is huge geysers, or fountains, of water vapor that shoot from the surface of the moon thousands of miles into space. Thirty of these spectacular jets were discovered by the Cassini spacecraft in 2005 (photo, right).

BTW

On Earth, a geyser is a hot spring that shoots water into the air. The geyser that shoots out the greatest distance is Steamboat, in Yellowstone National Park, in Wyoming. It doesn't erupt very often, but when it does, it can send hot water 300 feet in the air.

Mighty Mons

The **Olympus Mons** is an extinct volcano on Mars. At 15 miles high and about 375 miles across, it is thought to be the tallest and largest mountain in the solar system. Below is an outline of the state of Arizona placed over a photo of the volcano: They are about the same size! The Olympus Mons is a shield volcano, meaning it was built up from the flow of lava. It is 100 times larger than the largest shield volcano on Earth, Mauna Loa, in Hawaii.

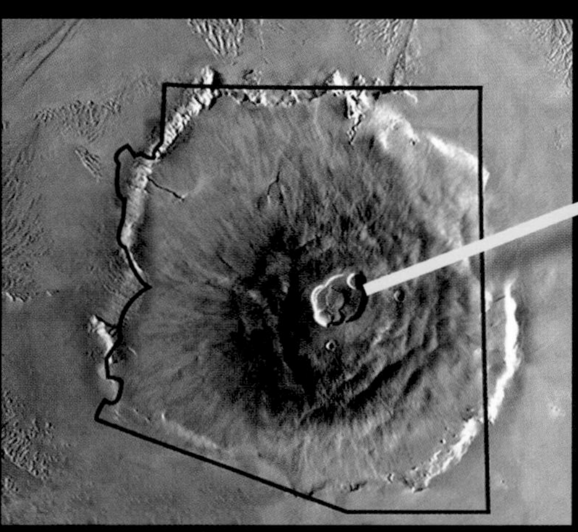

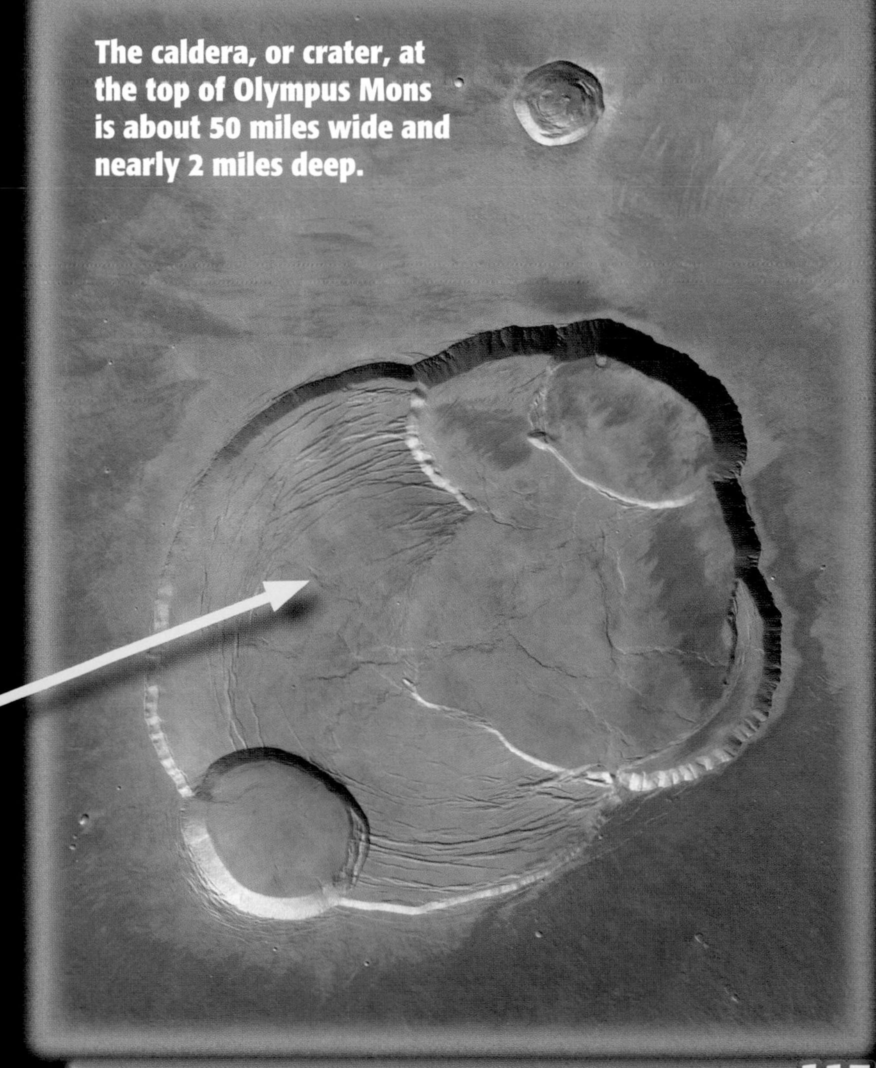

The caldera, or crater, at the top of Olympus Mons is about 50 miles wide and nearly 2 miles deep.

Making a Huge Impact

Over the last billion years, our planet has been hit by 130,000 meteorites large enough to make an impact crater at least two-thirds of a mile wide. (An impact crater is a hole or pit in the ground caused by a collision with an object from space.) So how come Earth isn't covered by craters like the moon? Wind, water, and changes in the Earth's surface have made craters disappear. But our planet has more visible scars from meteorites than you might realize. So far, scientists have found about 160 impact craters, scattered over every continent.

Incredible!

An asteroid more than 1,000 feet wide is on a near-collision course for Earth in 2029. Luckily, scientists say it will miss Earth by 18,600 miles—near enough to be able to see it with the naked eye. Now that's a close call!

Crater Down Under

One of the world's largest impact craters is the Wolfe Creek Crater, in Australia. Formed about 300,000 years ago, the crater is more than a half-mile across. The meteorite that made it weighed about 110 million pounds and left a hole as deep as a 40-story building. Over the years, sand filled much of the crater, which is now only about 180 feet deep, measured from its outer rim.

A Smash Hit

More than 200 million years ago, a 3-mile-wide meteor crashed into the Canadian province of Quebec. It left an enormous crater that filled with water, forming Manicouagan Lake. The lake forms a ring around a huge island of rock that rose up out of the crater. The **Manicouagan Crater** is 40 miles in diameter. It is so large that it can be seen from space, as shown in this photograph taken from the space shuttle *Columbia*.

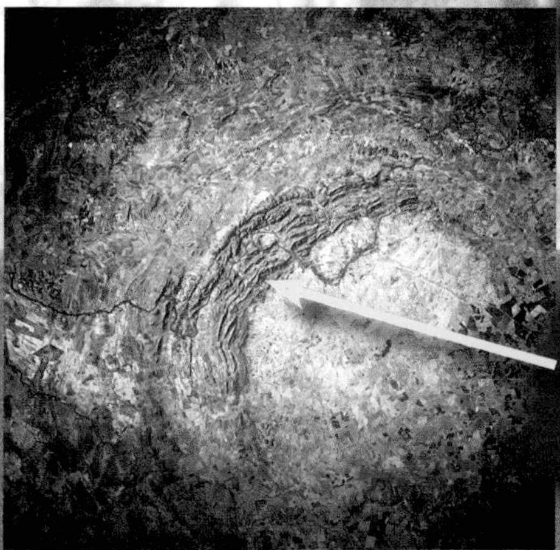

Incredible!

The largest, oldest impact crater on Earth is the **Vredefort crater**, in South Africa, made 2 billion years ago. The crater was about 180 miles across, but all that remains of it is the ring of hills (photo, left). It was caused by one of the largest meteorites ever to hit the Earth.

Here Comes the Sun

Say "melted cheese!" The sun is having its picture taken—again and again—by the Solar Dynamics Observatory (SDO). Launched into space by NASA in 2010, SDO was built to take millions of pictures of the sun for five years. The stunning images it's sending back show details of the sun never before seen.

Eye on the Sun

This illustration shows the **Solar Dynamics Observatory** (SDO) as it takes snapshots of the sun.

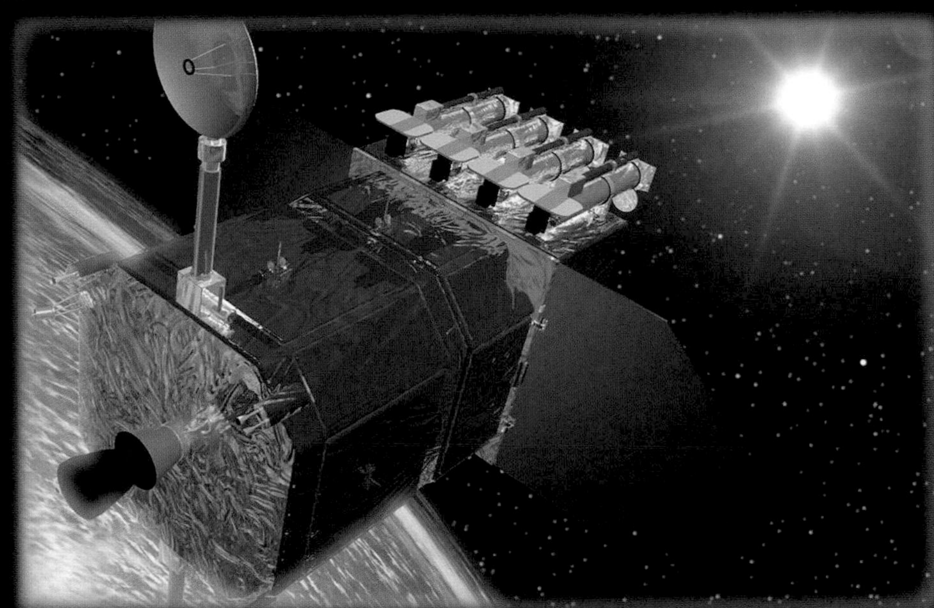

Incredible!

SDO produces enough data to fill a single CD every 36 seconds.

Turn Up the Gas

The 310-mile-thick surface of the sun is called the photosphere. Jets of gas, called **spicules**, constantly shoot off the sun's surface. Seen in the box in this photo, these bursts can move at speeds of 150,000 miles per hour. Spicules are about 6,000 miles long and reach a temperature of one million degrees. They transfer heat from the sun's surface to its atmosphere.

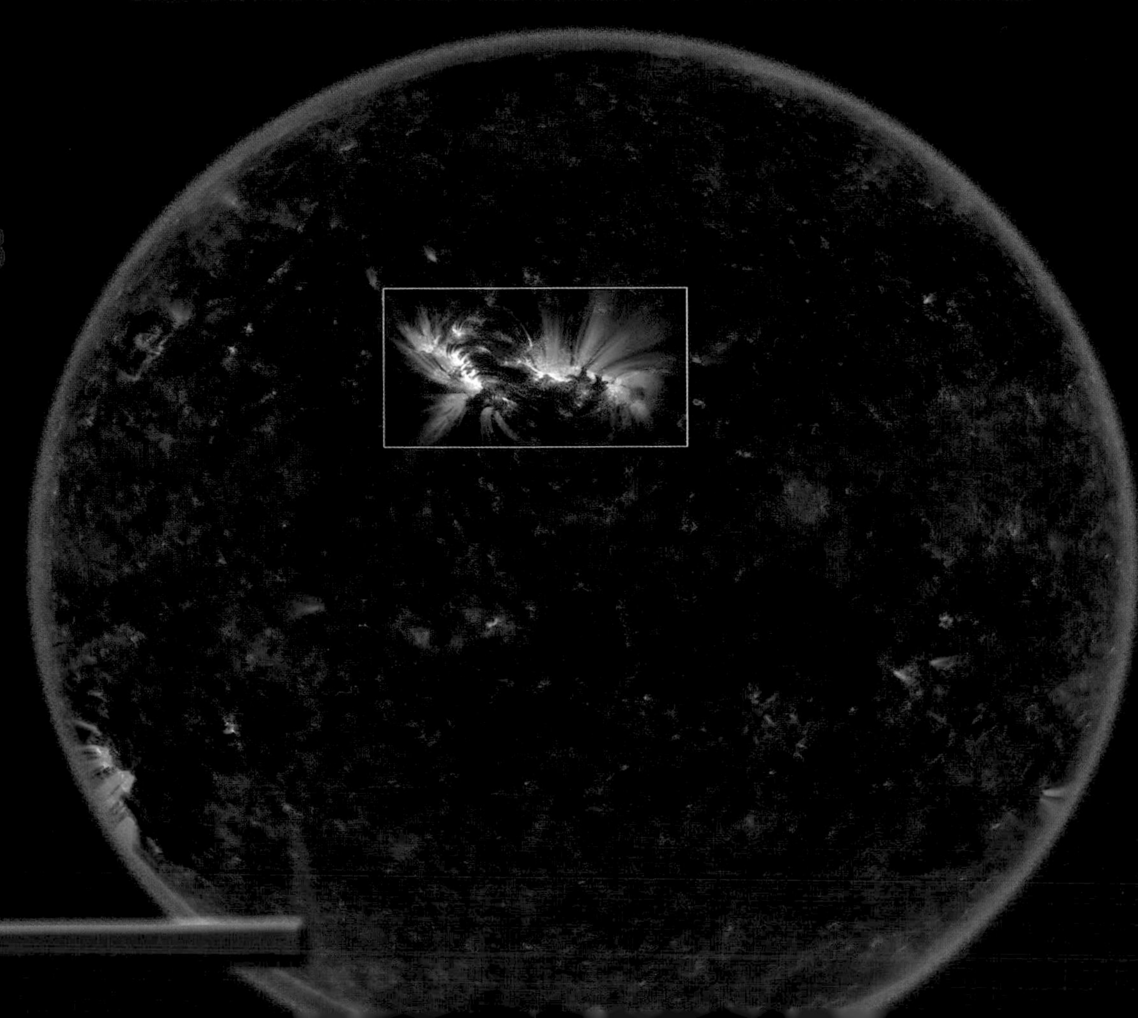

Solar Loop-de-Loop

A prominence is a cloud of hot gas that rises from the sun's surface. The magnetic field of the sun holds the gas in this loop-like shape until it collapses back onto the surface. Sometimes the eruption is so big and powerful, part of the prominence goes flying out into space. One recent prominence was 30 times the size of the Earth.

Earth

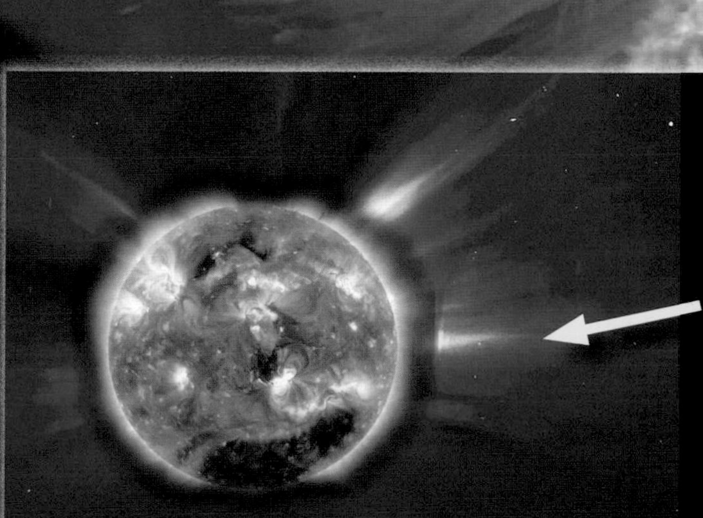

Show Some Flare

The yellow-white burst of light shooting out of the sun is a solar flare. A flare is a violent explosion in the atmosphere of the sun that produces incredible energy. It is caused by changes in the sun's magnetic field. This flare had a temperature of 35 million degrees.

Galactic Garbage

There's junk floating in space! About 500,000 pieces of space trash are circling Earth. These human-made objects are bits left behind from space launches that no longer have a purpose–anything from used rockets to tossed-away tools. Scientists fear these objects could smash into working satellites or spacecraft. NASA sent up a satellite to track the trash. It will give NASA a warning, so a satellite can be moved out of the way to avoid a collision. Meanwhile, it's a mess up there!

Look Out Below!

What goes up sometimes comes down. Gravity brought this fuel tank from a U.S. rocket back to Earth. The steel tank, which weighed about 550 pounds, landed harmlessly near Georgetown, Texas.

BTW

Most spacecraft on missions don't get hit very often by large pieces of space junk. But in 2009, an operating U.S. satellite collided with an out-of-use Russian satellite. Both satellites were completely destroyed.

This image shows space within 1,200 miles of the Earth's surface. It's the region most littered with space junk.

The dots represent pieces of space trash that are orbiting Earth. Space junk is anything from old spacecraft, rocket bodies and satellites, to blown-out rocket hatches, nuts and bolts, rubbish bags, and tiny bits of paint.

Most pieces of space junk are 4 inches or smaller. But there are tens of millions of particles smaller than a half inch. Most space trash orbits the Earth at speeds of more than 22,000 miles an hour. Moving at that speed, even a small object can cause damage if it hits something.

When junk is in an orbit less than 370 miles above Earth, it will fall back to the ground within a few years. If the trash is in an orbit at least 500 miles high, it may take decades to fall to Earth. Above 620 miles, it will orbit Earth for more than 100 years.

Chapter 8

Incredible Collections

What do barf bags, baseball cards, toilet seats, fortune cookie fortunes, toy frogs, hotel soap, and stamps have in common? They're all things that people collect. You might be a collector without knowing it. If you save space on your shelf for snow globes or Trolls or action figures or comics or…whatever, then you're a collector!

In This Chapter

- Kooky Cockroaches
- Matchless Matchsticks
- More than 1,500 Airsickness Bags

And Much More!

Incredible!

Patrick Acton builds and displays large models made out of wooden matchsticks. One of his most amazing creations is a replica of the space shuttle *Challenger*. He used 200,000 matchsticks on the spacecraft.

BTW

Erika Nelson creates the smallest versions of the largest things. This is her traveling museum—and the smallest version of it!

BTW

As a young boy, John Whitley started collecting souvenir plates from all 50 states. He also keeps adding to his collection with plates honoring U.S. Presidents. Whitley now has more than 2,000 plates.

Collector's Items

People collect all kinds of stuff. Some collections may seem silly, but whether it's old socks, yo-yos, tea bags, lunch boxes, or squirt guns, every item is important to its owner. That's why collectors often spend years hunting down objects to add to their treasure trove. Most of us collect something—even if it's dust! But some collections are way more unusual than others.

Pennies Saved

Ronald Dupont Jr.'s coin collection is flat-out fun. He collects pennies and quarters that have been crushed by machines found at fairs and theme parks. As the machine flattens and stretches the coin, it presses an image onto it. Dupont's collection includes coins that show Mickey Mouse, the MGM Tower of Terror, a T. rex, and the space shuttle.

Bag It!

There's nothing pleasant about getting airsick. But getting airsickness bags is great. At least it is for Steven Silberberg, who collects the bags and displays them online at the Air Sickness Bag Virtual Museum. Most of his 1,600 bags come from airlines, but there are bags made especially for cars, boats, trains, and helicopters. Prized possessions include an airsickness bag from the Vomit Comet, the plane that astronauts ride to experience weightlessness, and from the space shuttle. Airline pilots call barf bags "happy sacks." Silberberg calls them works of art.

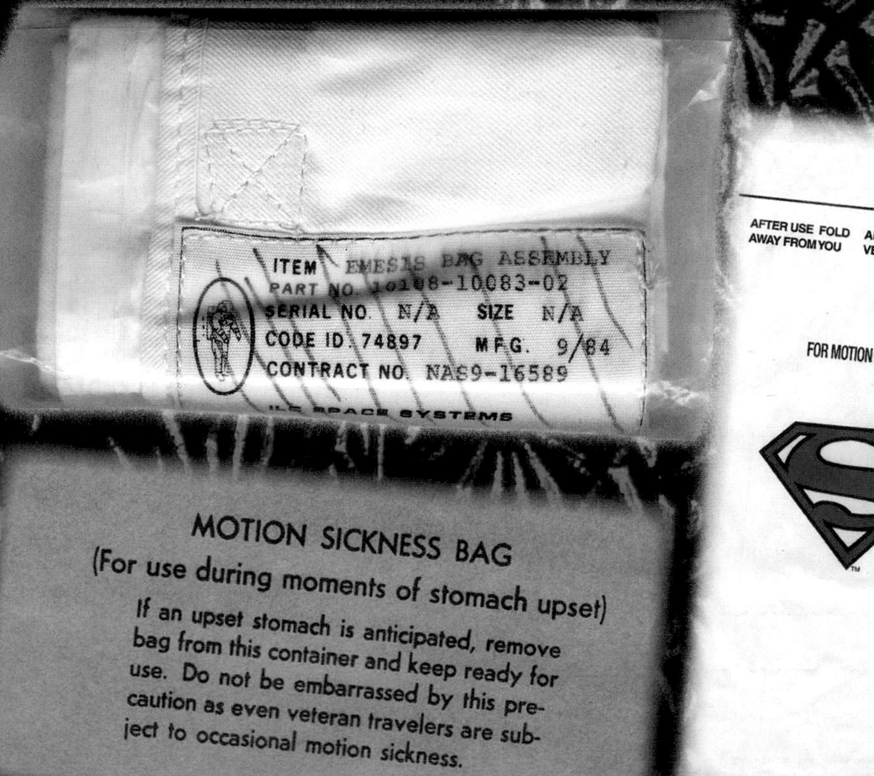

More Than Bones

Customers at The Bone Room in Berkeley, California, can buy human and animal skulls and skeletons, as well as claws, teeth, eggs, horns, and mounted butterflies. Also on sale are fossils of ancient animals, including dinosaurs. A fossil of oviraptor eggs goes for $3,000!

Burnt Offerings

Chefs should steer clear of Arlington, Massachusetts. That's the location of Deborah Henson-Conant's collection of burnt food. It began when she accidentally burned a pot of apple cider on her stove. She decided to keep it. These food foul-ups appear online, where you see burnt bagels, incinerated hot dogs, over-microwaved pizza, and much more.

Curious Collections

And you thought you've seen it all! Check out these collections of mind-boggling objects. Some treasures are in a truck that travels the roads, like a moving roadside attraction. Other incredible items on display are worthy of a natural history museum.

Actual Size

Small World

Kansas artist Erika Nelson has created a museum that tours in a bus. It's called The World's Largest Collection of the World's Smallest Versions of the World's Largest Things. Nelson makes and displays tiny versions of large roadside attractions. She's built Stonehenge out of miniature cars (above), and a small model of the Louisville Slugger Museum & Factory (right). She's also shrunk down the world's largest can of spinach and the biggest concrete pecan.

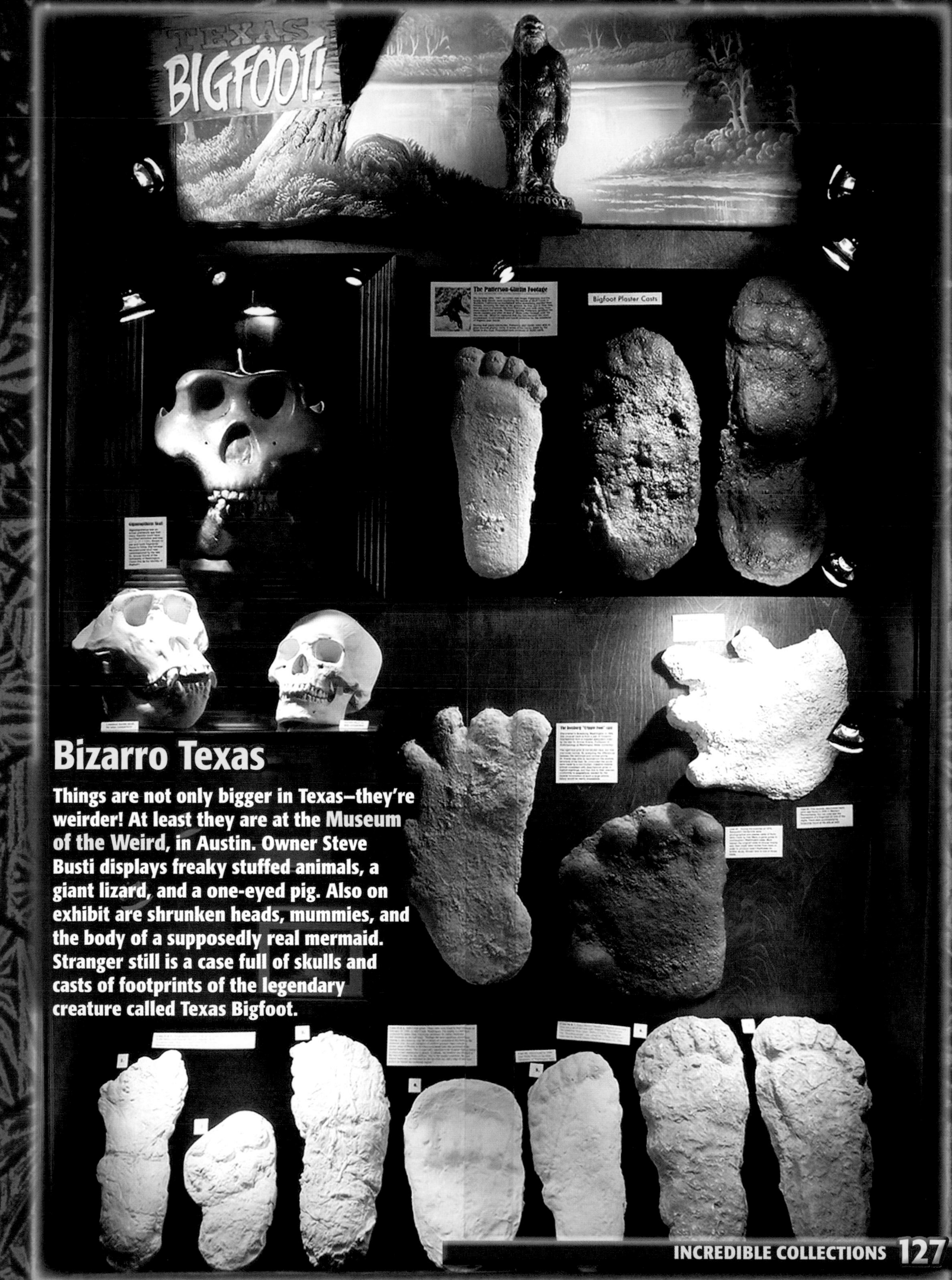

Bizarro Texas

Things are not only bigger in Texas—they're weirder! At least they are at the Museum of the Weird, in Austin. Owner Steve Busti displays freaky stuffed animals, a giant lizard, and a one-eyed pig. Also on exhibit are shrunken heads, mummies, and the body of a supposedly real mermaid. Stranger still is a case full of skulls and casts of footprints of the legendary creature called Texas Bigfoot.

Odd Museums

Some museums showcase great art, or important items of history, or the wonders of science. Other museums display objects that are odder (barbed wire, funeral carriages), sometimes downright peculiar (toilet bowls, butter), but always fascinating.

The Wheel Deal

People have been using in-line roller skates since 1819. That's one of the cool things you'll learn at **The National Museum of Roller Skating**, in Lincoln, Nebraska. It has the largest collection of roller skates in the world. There are exhibits about early American skates, in-line skates, roller hockey, speed skating, roller derby, and even ice skates. Roll on in!

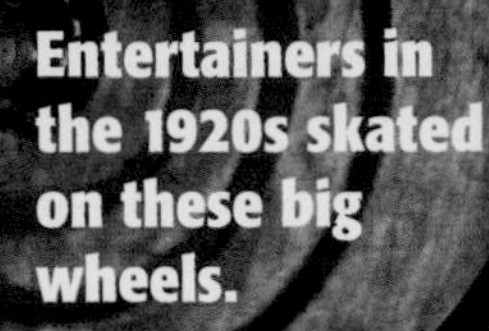

Entertainers in the 1920s skated on these big wheels.

Modern-day in-line skates (top) developed from older in-line skates, such as the three below it.

Roach Roundup

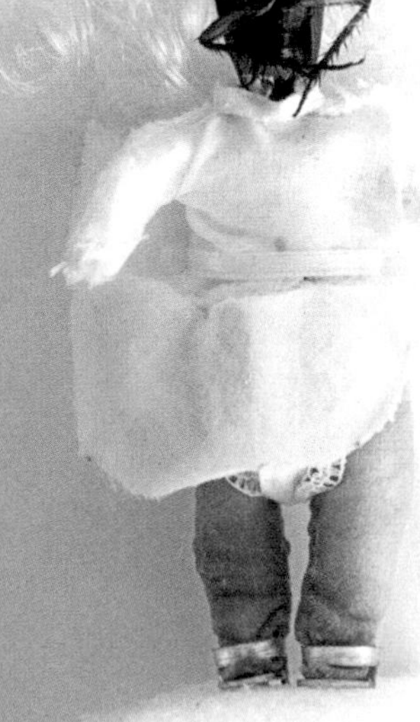

Cockroaches are tough little insects that have survived for millions of years. In their honor, Michael Bohdran started the **Cockroach Hall of Fame**, in Plano, Texas. Bohdran is a pest control expert, and The Pest Shop is part business and part museum. It displays dead roaches dressed up as celebrities, such as Elvis Presley and **Marilyn Monroe**, a famous movie actress. There are live roaches as well, including a Madagascar hissing cockroach.

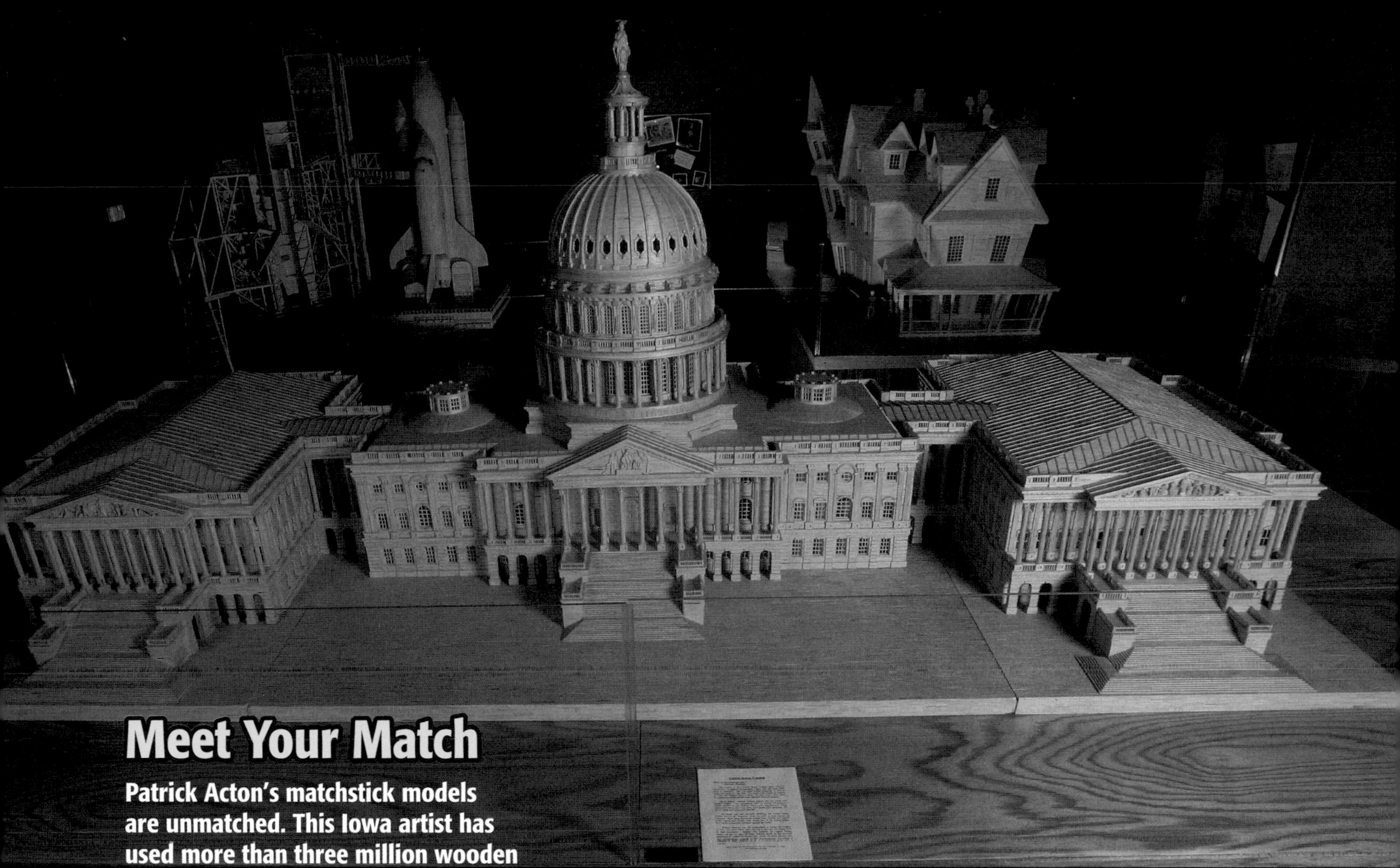

Meet Your Match

Patrick Acton's matchstick models are unmatched. This Iowa artist has used more than three million wooden matchsticks in gluing together 60 scale models of machines, buildings, and sculptures. (The tips that ignite have been removed from Acton's matchsticks.) His **Matchstick Marvels Tourist Center**, in Gladbrook, Iowa, includes a 13-foot-long scale model of the battleship USS *Iowa*, an *Apatosaurus*, the space shuttle *Challenger*, and a 12-foot model of the U.S. Capitol.

Incredible!

One of Acton's largest models is of **Hogwarts School of Witchcraft and Wizardry**, from the Harry Potter novels. It's made of 602,000 matchsticks. Gulping gargoyles!

Chapter 9
Incredible Jobs

Do you like reading? Building and fixing things? Math? Helping people? Sports? Computers? With some hard work, you can turn your interests and hobbies into a career. From architect to zookeeper, there are thousands of types of jobs in the world. And there are plenty of really out-of-the-ordinary jobs too. Here are some really cool careers.

In This Chapter

- Astounding Magician and Escape Artist
- Volcano Scientist
- LEGO® Master Builder

And Much More!

BTW

Donna O'Meara, a volcanologist, was trapped one night near the top of Stromboli volcano, in Italy, when it was erupting. The volcano made a huge explosion every half hour, yards from her head. But O'Meara made it through the night safely.

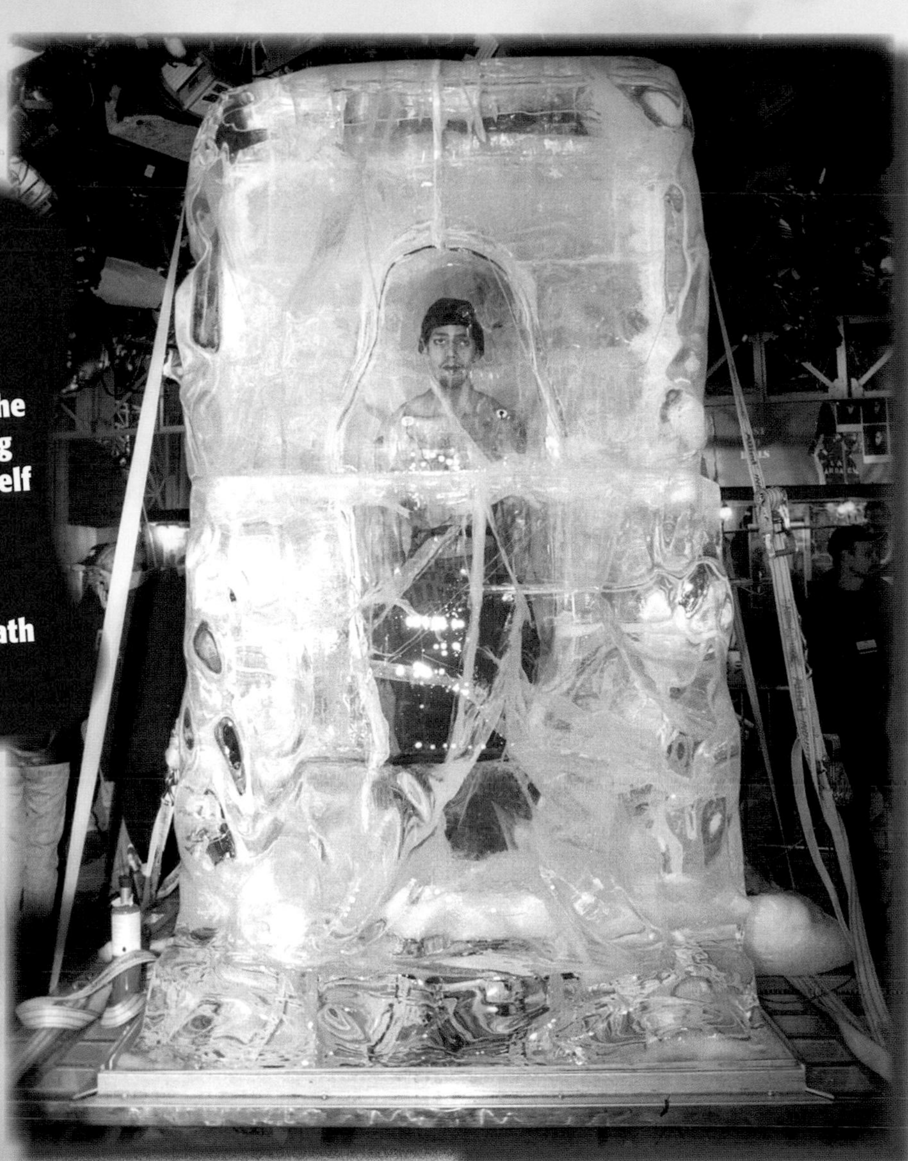

Incredible!

David Blaine is a famous magician and escape artist. One of his most breathtaking feats came in 2008 on the *Oprah Winfrey Show*. After breathing in pure oxygen, Blaine lowered himself into a sphere filled with water and held his breath for 17 minutes and 4.4 seconds. It was, at the time, the world's record for holding your breath after inhaling pure oxygen.

BTW

Mariann Asanuma was the first female LEGO® Master Model Builder at Legoland, in Carlsbad, California. Now she works on her own, constructing LEGO® models for companies for special events. Among Asanuma's awesome creations is a LEGO® Champagne bottle. She also built a LEGO® version of the Afro-American Cultural Center, located in Charlotte, North Carolina (shown here). To make it, Asanuma used between 7,000 and 8,000 plastic bricks!

They Wow the World

The goal of some jobs is to entertain people. Whether as a singer, an actor, or the creator of a video game, the point of this kind of work is to give an audience thrills and chills.

High-Wire Act

Philippe Petit knows how to keep his life in balance. Petit is a high-wire walker, able to walk across a thin cable stretched hundreds of feet in the air. Petit has performed his high-wire act many times, including 45 feet above the Niagara River, 225 feet above the street between the towers of Notre Dame Cathedral in Paris (photo), and between two buildings high above New York City streets. Born in France, he started out as a juggler and magician, but took to the tightrope as a teenager. Petit taught himself how to walk, sit, and even do somersaults on the high wire. One thing he has never done during a performance: fall.

Incredible!

In 1974, Philippe Petit performed his most famous feat. He walked on a steel cable stretched between the Twin Towers in New York City. The wire was 200 feet long and 1,368 feet above the ground. Despite windy conditions, Petit walked on the wire for 45 minutes, crossing back and forth between the towers eight times.

The Magic Man

David Blaine has spent his career amazing people. Blaine is a magician who can do card tricks that seem impossible. He also does jaw-dropping stunts that appear to risk his life. Blaine once put himself in a plastic box that was placed under a three-ton tank of water. He couldn't move, ate nothing, and drank a few tablespoons of water each day. Blaine stayed in the plastic box for seven days before coming out safe and sound. Another time, Blaine stood in a block of ice in New York City's busy Times Square for more than 63 hours. Thousands of passersby could see him through the ice. There's no trick to being a good magician—it's hard work!

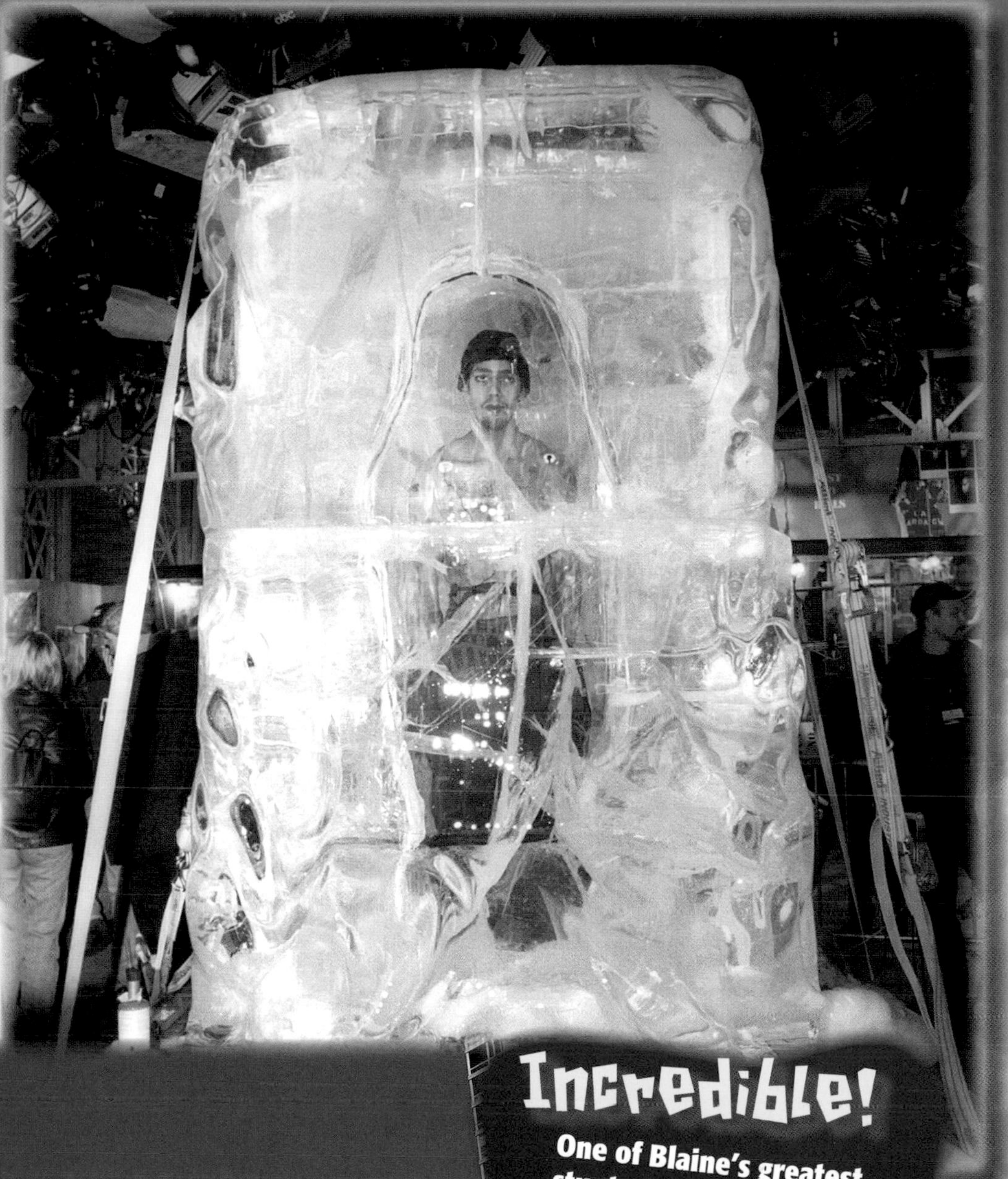

Incredible!

One of Blaine's greatest stunts was to escape from a gyroscope that hung 30 feet in the air. Blaine was chained to the gyroscope, which spun around eight times a minute. After 52 hours without eating or drinking, Blaine got out of his chains and jumped to the ground.

Thrilling Careers

Some jobs are exciting because they let you make discoveries about how the world works. These cool careers let you have great adventures—and learn a lot!

Donna O'Meara calmly takes photos of a 100-foot-tall "lavafall," which flows down the side of Kilauea, a volcano in Hawaii.

Volcanoes Are a Blast!

Donna O'Meara is a volcanologist, or a scientist who studies volcanoes. She and her husband have visited more than 100 of the 1,500 active volcanoes in the world. Studying a volcano up close is an exciting—and sometimes dangerous—job. When O'Meara arrives at an active volcano, she tries to get a local guide or geologist to give her and her husband background about the volcano. Next, they pick a site to set up camp. Once there, they put on gas masks, hard hats, and fire-resistant suits. Now they're ready to record the height, type, and time of each eruption. "The biggest challenge for a volcanologist is staying safe," says O'Meara. A person can be hurt at an erupting volcano, which can give off poison gas. O'Meara was always interested in science and nature. When she visited her first volcano, she was hooked on this force of nature. "I love my job!" says O'Meara.

From TIME FOR KIDS

Craving Caves

If you have a fear of tight spaces, then you probably don't want to be a supercave explorer. These scientists and daring adventurers climb thousands of feet underground, squeeze through tight holes, and plunge into cold underground rivers. Why? To reach very deep, unexplored caves. In these "supercaves," scientists are discovering unknown life forms. Some of the underground organisms are being used to create new antibiotics. The dangers of exploring supercaves are drowning, exposure to poison gases, and being buried under falling rocks. These dangers cause a lot of stress, which is why NASA is studying the teams that explore underground. They work in conditions similar to those astronauts will have on long space flights.

For the Record

The deepest cave in the world is the Krubera Cave, in Georgia, a country in central Asia. It is at least 7,188 feet deep—almost a mile and a half down. Cavers haven't explored it completely, so it might be even deeper.

Chapter 10

Incredible Technology

What would life be like without advances in technology? There would be no light bulbs, cars, computers, skateboards, cell phones, knives, forks, zippers, pens, doorknobs, bicycles, and HDTV, to name a few. In other words, life would be a lot harder—and a lot less fun.

In This Chapter

- A Bicycle That Bends
- Robots in Space
- A Real-Life Iron Man Suit
- The Biggest Airplane in the World

And Much More!

Incredible!

NASA has experimented with placing the body of a robonaut on top of a four-wheel rover. These "legs" might one day transport the bot across the surface of the moon or Mars.

BTW

The Martin Jetpack is supposedly safe for anyone to fly, but it has safety features—just in case: A parachute, a frame that absorbs the force of impact, and a shock absorber on its bottom.

Blast from the Past

In 1790, Thomas Jefferson introduced a system to record inventions. This eventually led to the U.S. Patent and Trademark Office, which keeps track of machines and gadgets, from the wacky to the incredible—like these doggy ear protectors!

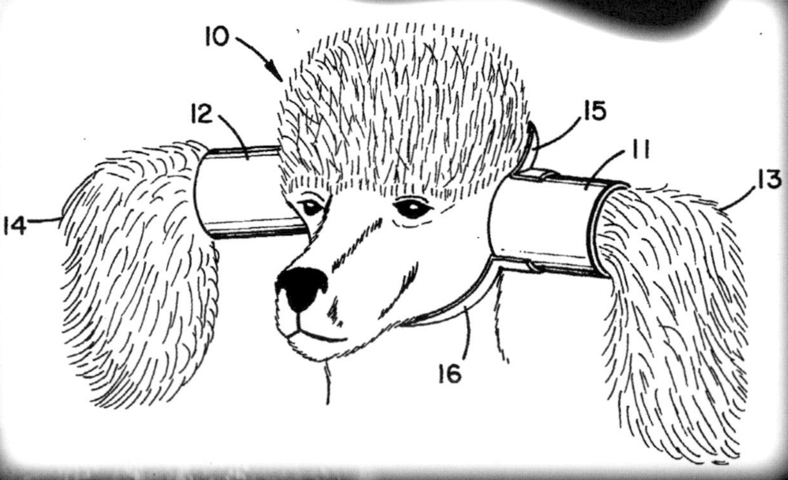

Fun and Games

Technology isn't just for making serious stuff. It can be used to make incredible products that you can play with. Technology can also inspire inventors to create toys and games. For example, Alfred Gilbert got the idea for inventing the erector set from watching a power-line tower being built. His toy was a miniature version of the girders and beams in the tower.

Watch It

The **Spy Net Video Watch** is the perfect gift for a future secret agent. The watch's high-tech features include a camera and microphone that record 20 minutes of video, four hours of audio, and can take up to 2,000 photos. The watch has a full-color screen that lets a user watch recorded videos. The info can even be downloaded onto a home computer.

SSIONS
3D CARDS
F.A.Q.
REALTECH
SPYNET
CAPTURE PHOTOS
UPLOAD & DOWNLOAD MISSIONS
SECRETLY RECORD VIDEO, AUDIO AND PICTURES
STEALTHILY RECORD AUDIO
VIDEO WATCH

Roach Robot

The **Hex Bug** is a robot cockroach that most people won't mind having in their homes. Its feelers are sensors that tell it to change direction when it runs into a wall or other object. The robot also scuttles away when it hears a loud noise—just like the real bug.

A Cool Cube

This **Rubik's Cube** has an inventive new twist: It's for people who are sightless. Each color side has its own symbol—for example, white has a circle and red has a square. Those who can see are able to solve this cube the usual way—by looking at the colors. People who are sightless can feel the raised symbols. They must use their sense of touch to make each face of the cube the same symbol.

Great Inventions

Inventors are always looking for ways to make our lives easier, greener, and a whole lot more fun. Breakthroughs in science and technology are bringing us some incredible inventions.

Superhero Suit

Have you ever dreamed of becoming a superhero? Dream no more. There's a real Iron Man suit, the **XOS 2**, that instantly changes the person wearing it. The suit enables a person to lift 200 pounds with ease or break slabs of wood with a single karate chop. It was designed to help the military with heavy lifting. One person in the suit could do the work of three soldiers.

Underwater Kite

The **Deep Green kite** doesn't fly in the sky. Instead, it is anchored to the ocean floor, and it swoops and dives totally underwater. As the ocean currents push and pull the kite, a turbine engine attached to it collects energy. Just one hour of the kite's work could supply about two weeks of power for the average home. The device can generate 800 times more power than if it were in the air.

Up, Up, and Away

It took him 30 years to develop it, and now Glenn Martin's invention is ready to take off. The **Martin Jetpack** allows its operator to fly 8,000 feet into the air. Unfortunately, you can't soar through the skies too long. The jetpack holds only about 30 minutes worth of fuel. It will sell for $100,000.

Robo-Guard

EMILY is not your typical lifeguard. She's a robotic, four-foot-long buoy that can swim through rough water at up to 24 miles per hour. Operated by remote control by a lifeguard, EMILY can be sent to swimmers in trouble.

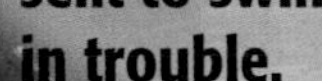

Green Machine

Say goodbye to gasoline! The **AirPod car** runs on—you guessed it—air power. That means this car won't pollute. A high-pressure air tank can fill the car in minutes. The three-wheeler can travel about 130 miles between fill-ups.

Ultimate Bicycles

Bicycles are a popular form of transportation: About 38 million people in the U.S. ride a bike at least six times a year, and about 15 million bikes are sold each year. Designers are coming up with wild ideas for amazing new types of bicycles. You might be riding one in the near future.

Bendable Bikes

It looks like a normal bike. But at the press of a lever, the two rigid tubes that serve as the frame of the bike become **bendable**. The rider can wrap the bike around a pole and lock it onto itself. To ride the bike, simply press the lever, and the tubes become rigid again.

BTW

In the Netherlands, 30 percent of all trips are on bicycles.

In the Fold

This electric bike can be ridden—or carried. The **VW bik.e** can quickly fold up into the size of a tire. And like a tire, it can fit in the trunk of a car. When a driver reaches a destination (such as a scenic trail), she can park the car, unfold the bike, and pedal away.

Wood You Ride This?

Most bikes are a green way of traveling because they don't cause pollution or use up resources—except for the metal parts. The **Xylon** (*zi*-lahn) is more green than most bikes. The frame of the bike is made of wood, instead of plastic or metal. Although wood seems low-tech, the design of the wood frame is completely cool.

Incredible!

The greatest bike race in the world is the Tour de France. The annual race is three weeks long and covers on average 2,200 miles, mostly through France.

Just Plane Amazing!

Talk about a jumbo jet! The Airbus A380 is the biggest commercial airplane ever built. It's a double-decker behemoth that can carry as many as 853 people. The Airbus A380 is nicknamed the Green Giant because of its size and the fact that it is designed to reduce its impact on the environment. To make taking off and landing possible, the Airbus A380 has 22 wheels. Are you ready for takeoff? Please fasten your seatbelts!

A camera on the tail of the plane gives passengers and crew a view outside on takeoff, during the flight, and while landing.

239 feet

The wings and body of the plane are made of aluminum, plus plastic mixed with glass and carbon fibers. These light materials reduce the weight of the airplane and save fuel.

BTW

The Airbus A380 can travel 9,200 miles without needing to refuel. It can fly non-stop from New York City to Hong Kong, a city on the east coast of China.

261 feet

The wingspan of the Airbus A380 is longer than the distance the Wright Brothers' plane traveled on its first flight, in 1903.

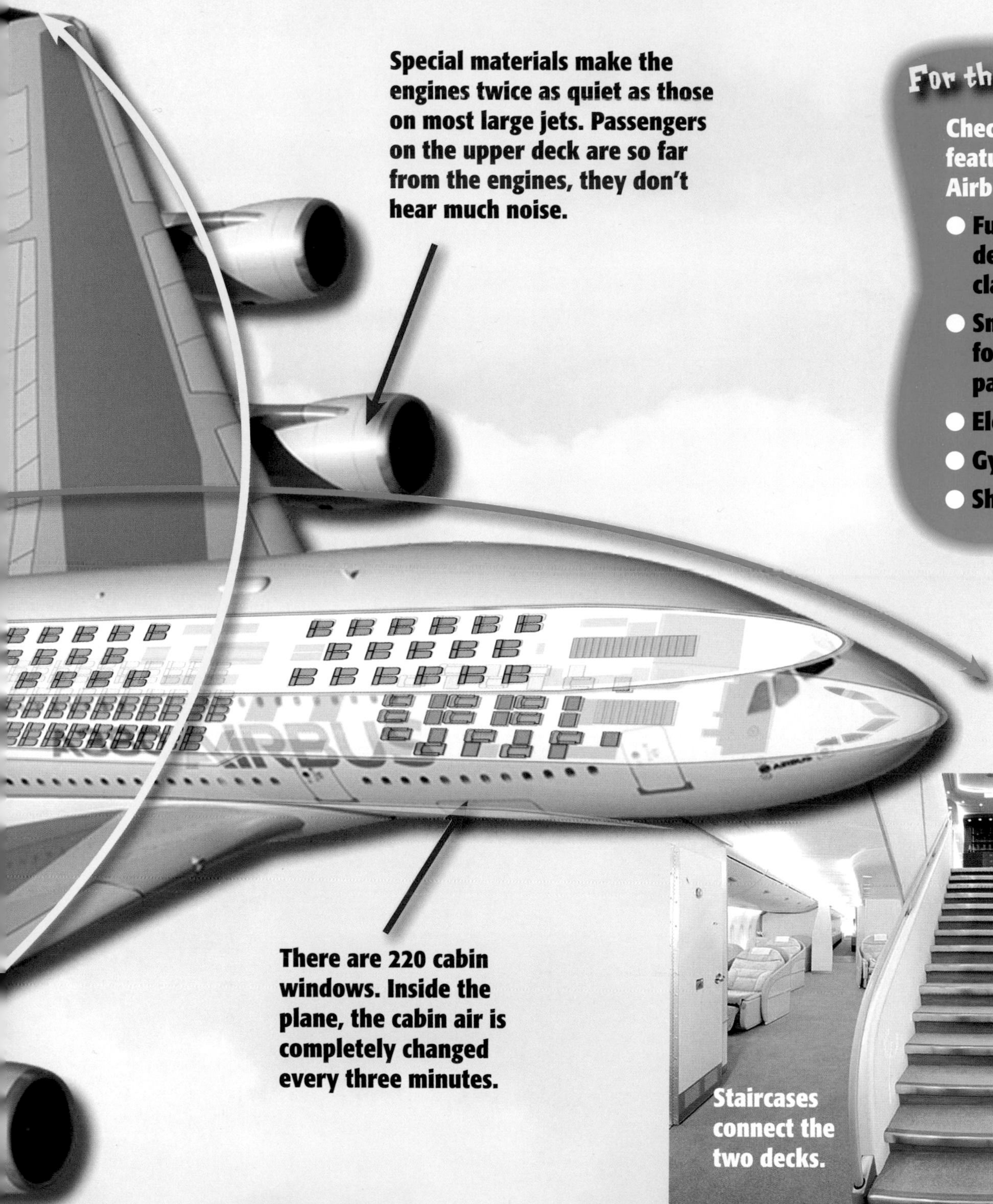

Special materials make the engines twice as quiet as those on most large jets. Passengers on the upper deck are so far from the engines, they don't hear much noise.

For the Record

Check out the cool features in some Airbus 380s:

- Full-size beds and desks in the first class sections
- Small private rooms for individual passengers
- Electronic art gallery
- Gym and casinos
- Showers

There are 220 cabin windows. Inside the plane, the cabin air is completely changed every three minutes.

Staircases connect the two decks.

Incredible!

The A380 is nearly 240 feet long—that is about the length of five schoolbuses.

Which One Is Real?

Got a great idea for an invention? You probably should apply for a patent then. A patent is a document that proves an idea or invention is yours and can't be copied by others. For more than 200 years, the U.S. Patent and Trademark Office has given patents to inventions that it judges new and useful, although some very odd devices have received patents. All these patents are real—except one. Can you guess which is the made-up patent? The answer is upside down below.

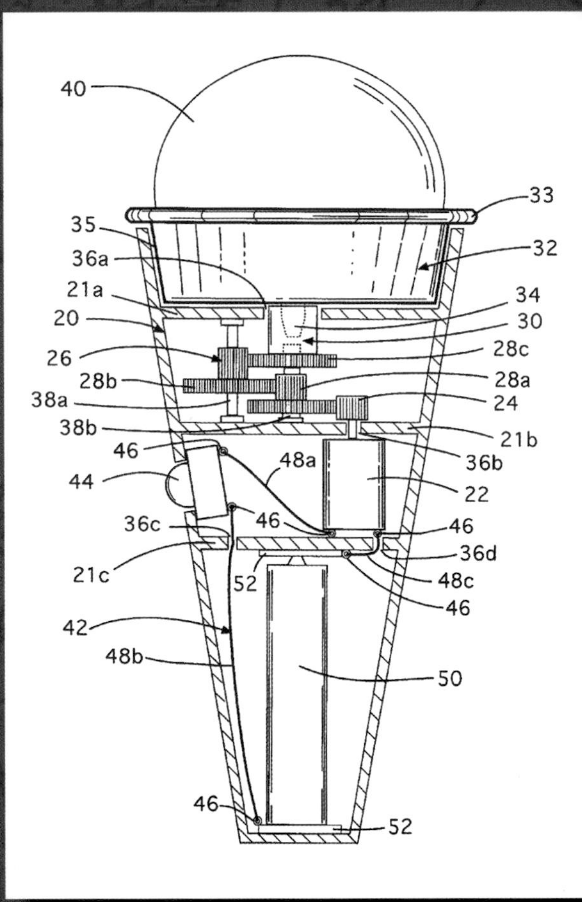

1. Motorized Ice Cream Cone

U.S. Patent No. 5,971,829 • 1999

Sometimes when you're eating ice cream, you're just too tired to turn the cone. That's when this device comes in handy. Inside the housing is a battery-operated motor. It rotates a cup filled with ice cream (or some other soft food). The ice cream rotates while your tongue stays in one place.

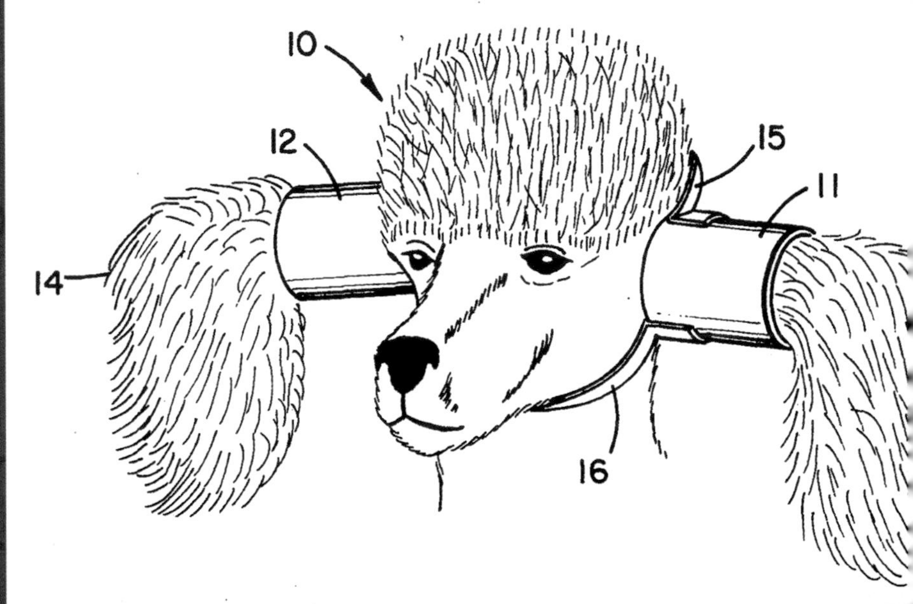

2. Animal Ear Protectors

U.S. Patent No 4,233,942 • 1980

The inventor of this device worries about dirty dogs. The problem is, when droopy-eared dogs eat, their ears can touch their mouths or the food and get soiled. This device covers each ear with a little protective cap and at the same time keeps the ears away from the dog's mouth and bowl of chow.

BTW

The first U.S. patent was given in 1790. It was for a way to improve the making of soap.

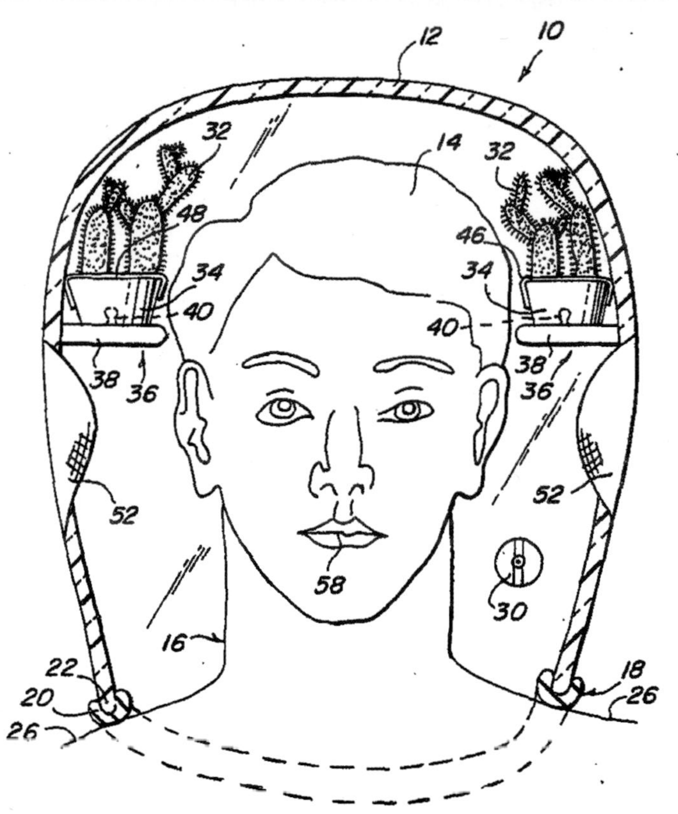

3. Greenhouse Helmet

U.S. Patent No. 4,605,000 • 1986

People breathe in oxygen and breathe out carbon dioxide, while plants do the opposite. This device uses that process to clean the air you breathe. It's a glass dome that is worn over the head and sealed around the neck. Attached to the inside are small plants. The person breathes in the fresh air from the plants, and the plants take in the person's carbon dioxide.

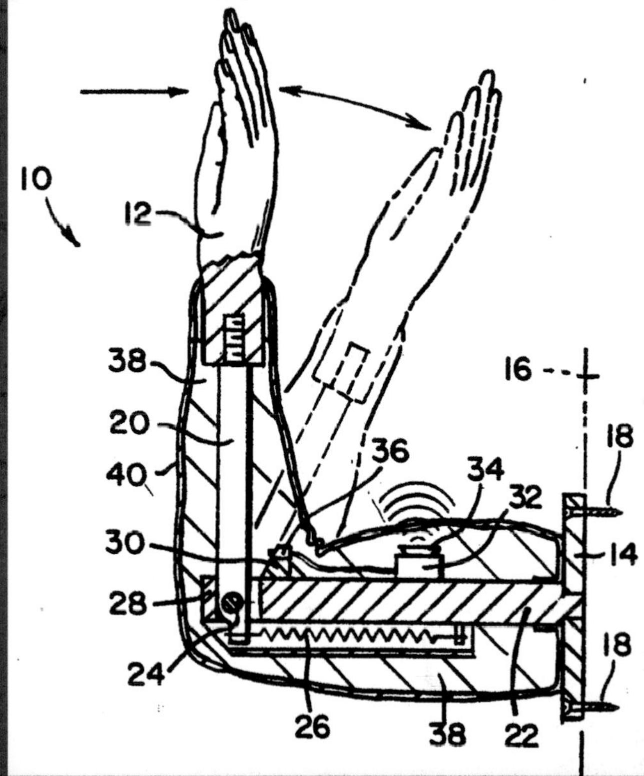

4. High-Five Machine

U.S. Patent No. 5,356,330 • 1993

There are times a person wants to high-five someone but there's nobody around. It can happen when you're alone while getting a high score in a computer game or watching a sports event on TV. This device solves the problem: It's an artificial hand attached to a spring that moves forward at the push of a button to slap your hand.

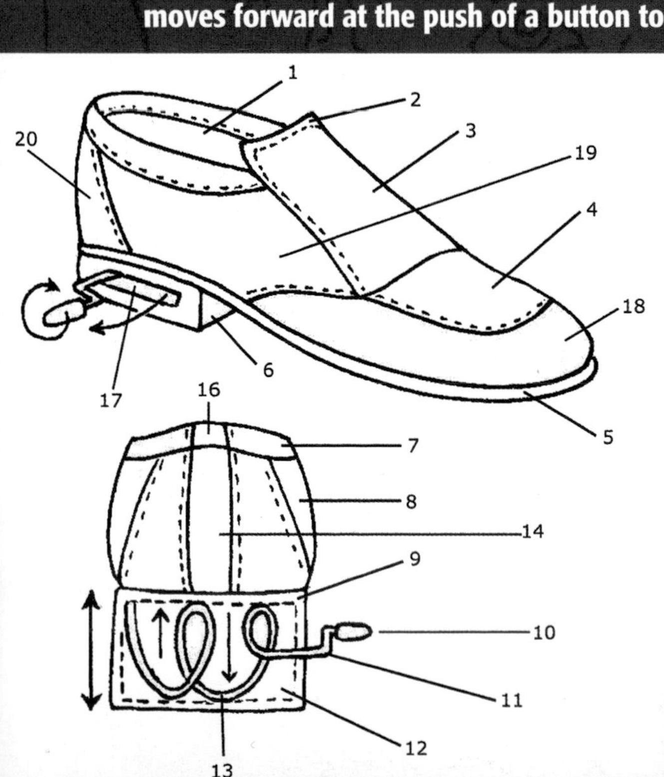

5. Hand-Cranked Lift Shoes

U.S. Patent No. 1,234,742 • 2007

These shoes come with a small crank that goes into an opening in the heel. When the crank is turned, the heel stretches out and adds up to five inches to the wearer's height. The device allows a person to see over fences and over people's heads at parades and other events.

Answer: The fake is #5.

Green Giants

Buildings are getting bigger—and greener. Because Earth's environment is being threatened by pollution and the waste of its resources, more and more architects around the world are creating buildings that use renewable energy sources and recycled materials. Even the largest, most spectacular structures are being designed to save energy and be eco-friendly.

Wonder-fall

The 2016 Summer Olympic Games will be held in Rio de Janeiro, Brazil. Brazil plans on constructing a building to impress visitors. One design being considered is the Solar City Tower. During the day, solar panels on the 344-foot-tall tower would produce electricity for Rio and the Olympic Village. At night, any leftover electricity will be used to pump seawater into the tower. The water will be released to drive turbines and generate more electricity for the city. Some of the water will also be sent over the side of the tower to create a huge waterfall.

A Mammoth Building for Moscow

Now this is a mega mall! The project is planned for Moscow, the capital of Russia. The spiral-shaped building is designed to be 1,476 feet high and hold 30,000 people. It will have hotels, apartments, offices, shops, museums, and theaters. Solar panels and wind turbines on the building will generate electricity. The building will be covered by two layers of tent-like "skin." They are designed to keep the building cool in the summer and warm in the frigid Moscow winter.

It's Good Being Green

Bank of America Tower is the second tallest building in New York, but it may be tops in saving energy. The building was made from recycled materials, and the waste from construction was also recycled. The building captures and reuses rainwater. Some of its toilets don't use water, which saves about 5 million gallons in a year. The cooling system makes ice, which is used to cool the building during hot days. If that wasn't enough, the air inside the building is cleaned before it's sent back outside the building. Now that's green.

Green Buildings in the World

1. Alamaden Tower, San Jose, California
2. India Tower, Mumbai, India
3. William J. Clinton Presidential Library, Little Rock, Arkansas
4. Robert Redford Building, Santa Monica, California
5. Rochester Institute of Technology, University Services Center, Rochester, New York

Source: Forbes.com

BTW

One of the most famous buildings constructed for the Olympics is the National Stadium, in Beijing, China. Built for the 2008 Summer Games, it's nicknamed the Bird's Nest.

Bring on the Bots

Creating robots that can act like humans seems more science fiction than fact. But over the years, scientists have taken the challenge of building a better bot. Today, robots are more life-like than ever.

Hardworking Robot

The **EMIEW2 robot** is the perfect office helper. Need a document delivered? No problem! It can also guide visitors to their destinations—at a top speed of four miles per hour. The nearly three-foot-tall bot can identify different human voices and respond to commands. One day, it may serve as a receptionist or a security guard.

Robo-Teachers

Some students in South Korea have a new language instructor: an **English-teaching robot**. The bots help students practice speaking English. South Korea hires 30,000 foreigners to teach English. The robo-teachers are helping to solve a shortage of English teachers. Could robots replace human teachers one day?

Incredible!

Researchers have found that students are more relaxed around robot teachers than real ones. The kids don't mind making mistakes in front of the robots.

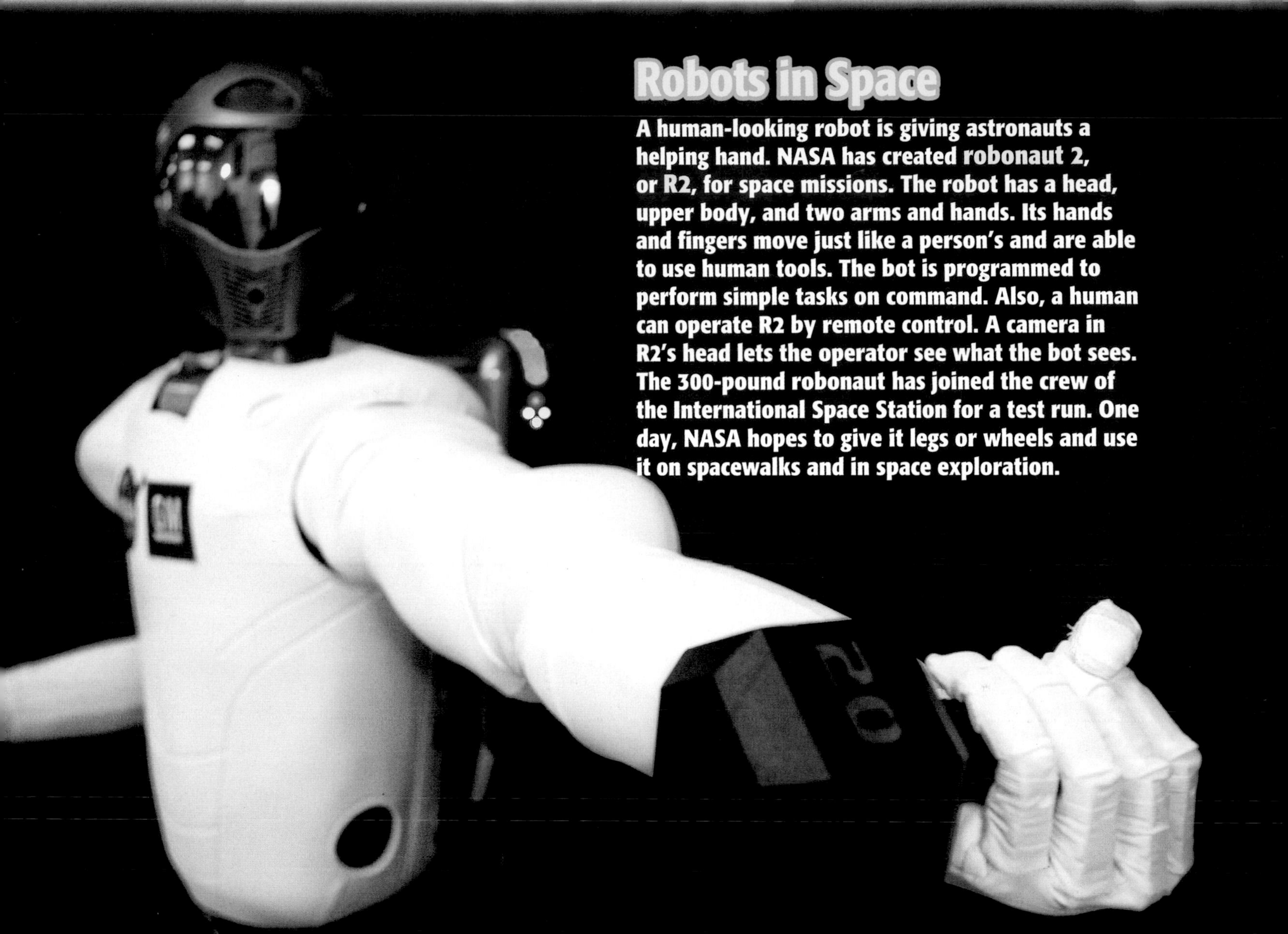

Robots in Space

A human-looking robot is giving astronauts a helping hand. NASA has created robonaut 2, or R2, for space missions. The robot has a head, upper body, and two arms and hands. Its hands and fingers move just like a person's and are able to use human tools. The bot is programmed to perform simple tasks on command. Also, a human can operate R2 by remote control. A camera in R2's head lets the operator see what the bot sees. The 300-pound robonaut has joined the crew of the International Space Station for a test run. One day, NASA hopes to give it legs or wheels and use it on spacewalks and in space exploration.

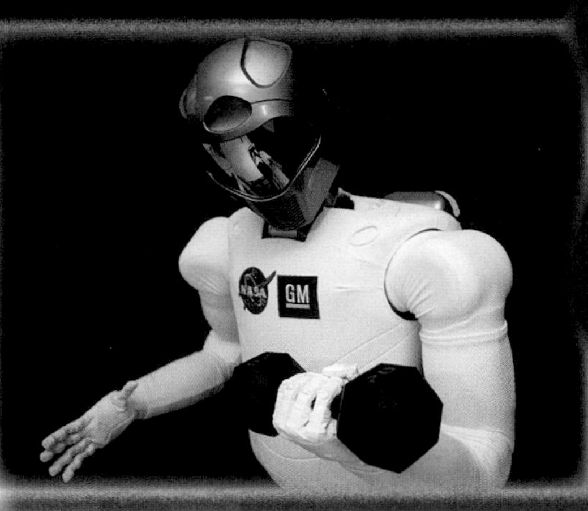

BTW

Robonaut 2 thinks with its stomach. Because its head is full of cameras, the bot's control center was placed in the lower part of its body.

Chapter 11 Incredible Human Body

All of our bodies have more or less the same parts that work the same way. Of course, there are lots of parts and the work they do is incredibly complicated. Even a computer is like a simple toy compared to the design of the human body. Our insides and outsides are so astonishing!

In This Chapter

- How Heavy Is a Brain?
- A Third Eyelid in Humans
- Making New Lungs
- A Look Inside the Body

And Much More!

Incredible!

Body Worlds is an astonishing traveling exhibit that shows the inside of real, specially preserved bodies. The bodies are placed in realistic poses, doing such activities as dancing, skateboarding, and playing soccer. This soccer player's muscles are visible to viewers, including the powerful thigh muscles used to kick the ball.

BTW

How do you communicate when your brain is working but parts of your body are paralyzed? The EyeWriter might be the perfect tool. It lets people who can't speak or move their arms write and draw by using their eyes. The glasses track the user's eye movements, and a special computer translates the movements into lines or words on a screen.

Blast from the Past

Humans have fairly small toes compared to most animals. Scientists think smaller feet helped hungry humans hunt animals over long distances.

An Inside Look

Few of us get to see what's under our skin—unless you happen to visit *Body Worlds*, an exhibit which tours the U.S. Visitors get to see the insides of real bodies that have been preserved through a special process, giving people an up-close view of what makes humans so special.

Incredible!

Body Worlds was created by a German scientist, Gunther von Hagens. In 1977, he developed a method to preserve human bodies called Plastination. The process works by first replacing natural fluids in a body with liquid plastic. Next, the body is put in a lifelike pose with the use of clamps and wires. Finally, light, gas, or heat is used to harden the plastic so the body keeps its shape.

Head Case

There's a lot going on inside everyone's head. It contains the major sense organs, including the eyes, ears, taste buds, and the nerves in the nose that detect smells. It holds the mouth and the top of the tube that leads to the stomach and lungs. The skull also contains the brain, which is made of 100 billion nerve cells called neurons.

Being Handy

Inside the lower arm and hand is a spectacular network of three types of blood vessels: veins, arteries, and capillaries (*cap*-uh-lair-ees). Arteries deliver oxygen and nutrients to the body's cells. Waste material from the cells is carried away by veins. Hair-thin capillaries connect veins and arteries.

What a Kick!

Visitors to Body Worlds can see the skeletal muscles of a soccer player. **Skeletal muscles**—red areas in the photo—are muscles that move bones and give the body its shape. There are about 640 skeletal muscles in a body. Among the most powerful are the thigh muscles, which the player uses to kick the ball.

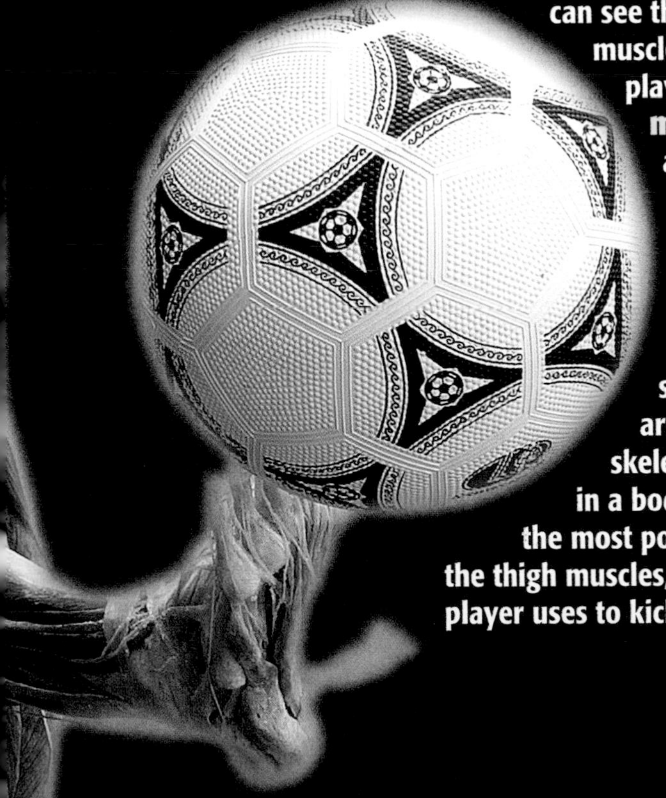

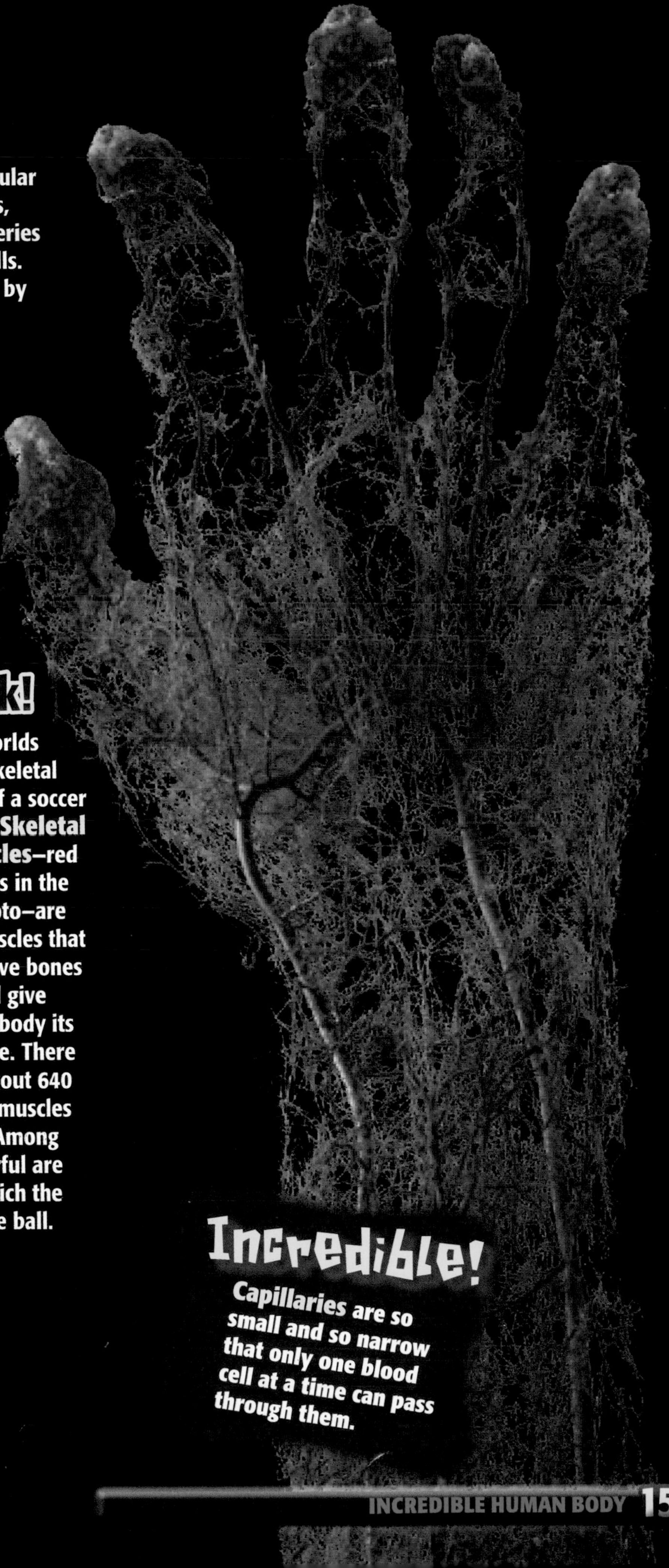

Incredible!

Capillaries are so small and so narrow that only one blood cell at a time can pass through them.

Technology for Life

Researchers are always looking for new ways to keep us healthy. Advances in technology are helping people live longer—and better—lives.

Breathing Easier

Researchers have re-created the lung of a rat in a lab. The lung is able to breathe in and out almost as well as a normal rat's lungs. The final goal of the scientists is to copy the feat on a larger scale: to replace enough human lung tissue to help patients with lung diseases.

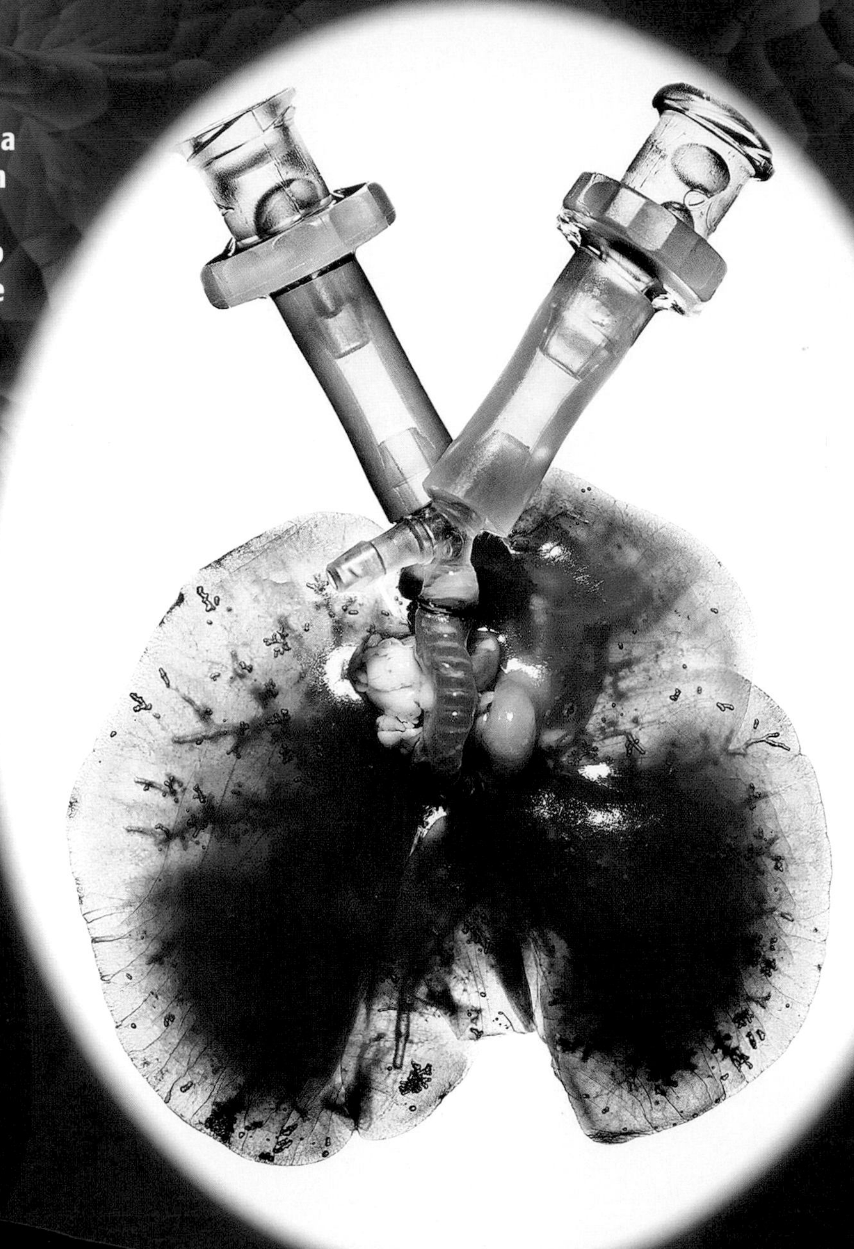

Creating a Super Salmon

Salmon not only tastes good, it's good for you. The fish contains a kind of oil that helps prevent heart disease. Because of its popularity, wild salmon is being fished out of existence. Most of the salmon we now eat is farmed, not caught. The problem is that it takes three pounds of feed to grow one pound of salmon. One company's solution is to splice in a gene from Chinook salmon with DNA from an eel-like creature called an ocean pout. The new salmon can grow twice as fast, making them easier to farm—and producing more of them to eat.

Buzz Off

The **mosquito** is a little insect that causes big problems. It is responsible for spreading many diseases, especially one called malaria. A man named Nathan Myhrvold is trying to do something about it. He is developing a laser that can zap mosquitoes without harming other insects or humans.

Incredible!

Each year, mosquitoes cause 250 million cases of malaria.

One Step at a Time

The makers of eLEGS hope to help people with paralyzed legs stand and walk on their own. The device is made up of **robotic legs** and crutches. It uses a special computer program to "read" the wearer's arm movements through the crutches. It causes the legs to move in a natural motion.

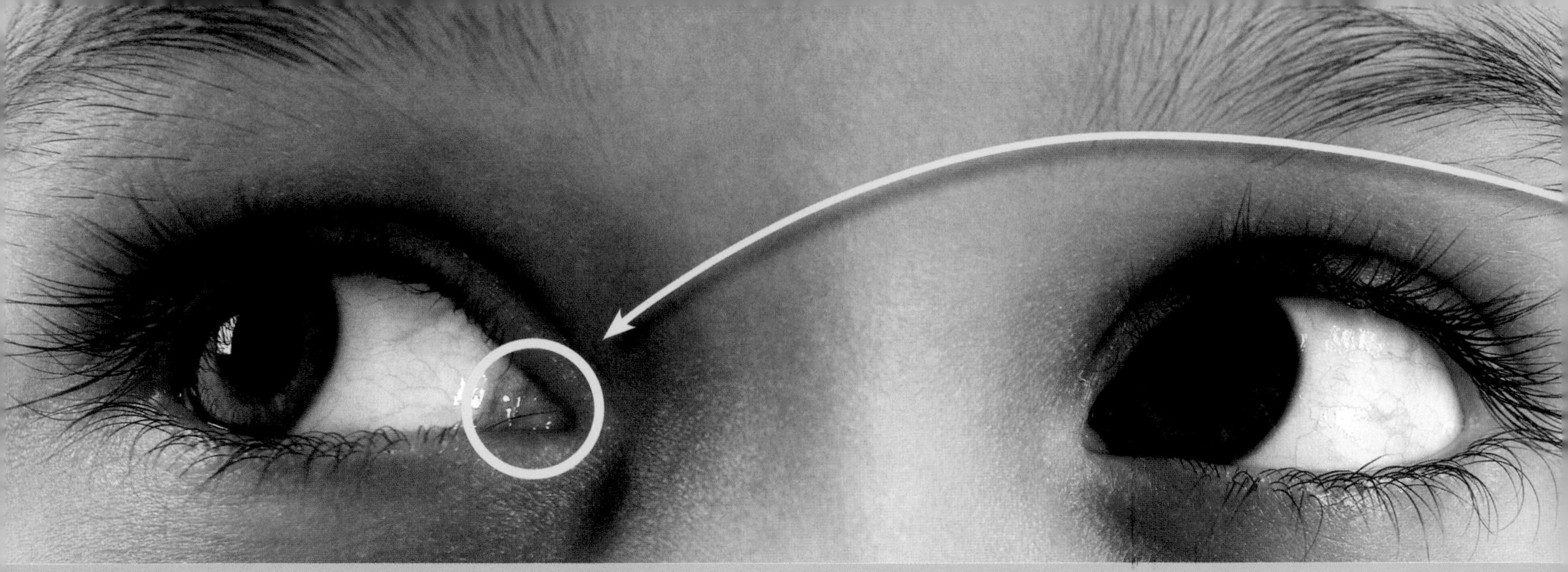

Who Needs These Body Parts?

The body works like a well-oiled machine. It has lots of parts and they all seem to have a function to keep us healthy. Or do they? It turns out there are a few parts of our body that are just along for the ride. Some of them may have had a use in the past, but they no longer do much of anything. What are these amazing slackers?

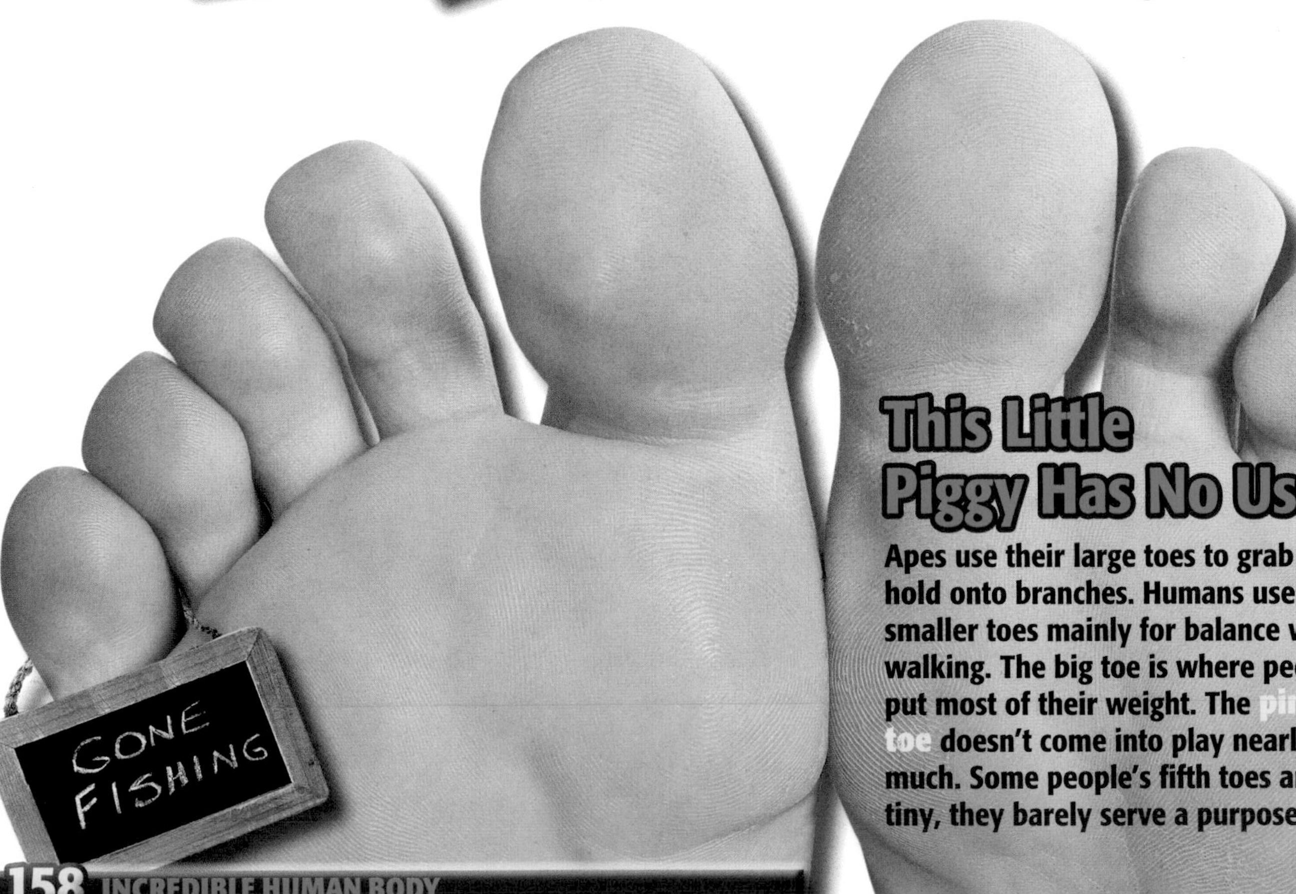

This Little Piggy Has No Use

Apes use their large toes to grab and hold onto branches. Humans use their smaller toes mainly for balance when walking. The big toe is where people put most of their weight. The pinky toe doesn't come into play nearly as much. Some people's fifth toes are so tiny, they barely serve a purpose.

Eye See You

Gently pull open the eyelids at the inside corner of your eye and you'll see something amazing: a **third eyelid**. It's a small leftover piece of a nictitating (*nick*-tuh-tate-ing) membrane. Many animals have this membrane, which they draw horizontally across the eyes. The membrane protects an animal's eyeballs while their eyes are open. For us, it just takes up space.

Incredible!

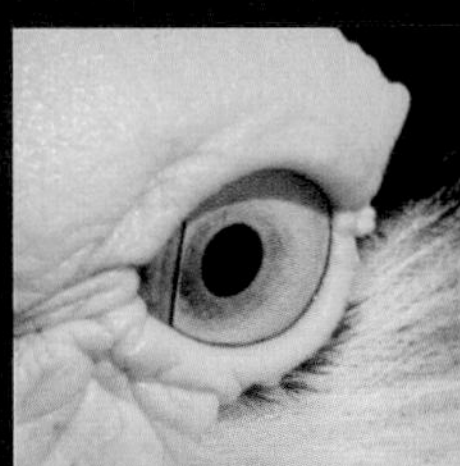
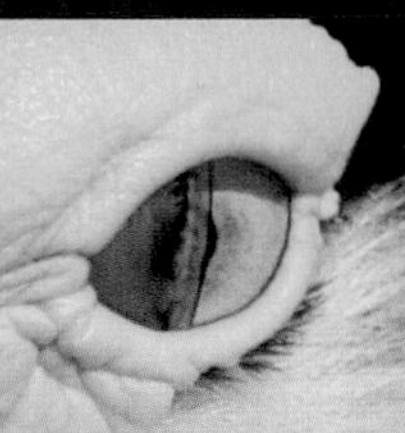
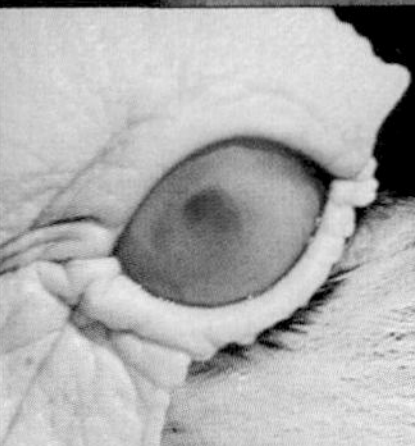

The masked lapwing is native to Australia. Like many birds, it has a nictitating membrane, or third eyelid, that slides horizontally across the eye. The see-through membrane protects the bird's eyes and also keeps the peepers clean and moist.

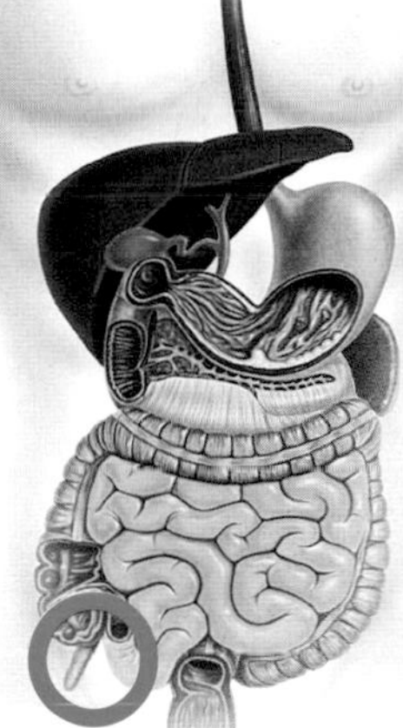

Waste of Space?

Most people think of the **appendix** only when it has to be removed because it is infected. This narrow little tube attached to the small intestine might have helped early humans digest cellulose, a tough part of a plant. In those ancient days, people probably ate more plants than animals. Modern humans can't digest cellulose. To be fair, the appendix does produce some white blood cells. But mostly it is useless.

The Tooth Hurts

Ancient humans had to eat lots and lots of plants to get enough nutrients to stay alive. For those early humans, large jaws and an extra set of molars came in handy (or mouthy!) to chew tough vegetation. Those extra molars are our **wisdom teeth**. We no longer have big jaws—and we no longer need wisdom teeth to eat food. In fact, many people don't have them or have them pulled—and they have no problems eating.

A Hairy Situation

Hair can be helpful: On the brow it keeps sweat from our eyes and cuts down on the sun's glare. Eyelashes keep dust out of our eyes. Hair on the head protects our head from the sun. But **hair on the body** doesn't do much. Millions of years ago, people were probably covered with hair. It kept them warm and kept insects away. Now we have clothes to keep us warm.

The Incredibly Amazing

The human body is made up of about 100 trillion cells. Those cells make up an astounding collection of organs and other body parts, all of which keep us alive and well. How much do you know about what's happening on the inside and outside of the body? Take this quiz to find out. (The answers are printed upside down below.)

1 Nails on fingers and toes are both made of keratin (*kair*-a-tin), the same substance hair is made of. But there are differences between fingernails and toenails. If you are right-handed, the nails on your right hand grow faster than those on your left. It's the other way around if you're left-handed. On the other hand (other foot?), toenails grow at the same rate on both feet. Also, fingernails and toenails grow at different rates. Which grows faster?

a. Fingernails

b. Toenails

2 The skin is the largest organ in the body. How big is it?

a. 8 square feet—about the size of four large pizza boxes

b. 20 square feet—slightly smaller than the average door of a room

3 The brain of a medium-size dog weighs about three ounces—about as much as a lemon. A grasshopper's brain is one-thousandth of an ounce—about as heavy as a grain of rice. The adult human brain weighs about as much as a

a. Head of iceberg lettuce—about $1^1/_2$ pounds

b. Cantaloupe—about 3 pounds

4 Iron in the body is found in red blood cells and is also stored in different organs. Altogether, there's enough iron in the human body to make

a. One small nail

b. A pair of scissors

5 The human body is about 60 percent water. An average person drinks how much water in a lifetime?

a. About 16,000 gallons

b. About 38,000 gallons

Human Body Quiz

6 What part of the day is your **eyesight** the sharpest?

a. In the morning

b. In the middle of the day

7 **Beards** are the fastest growing hair. If the average man never cuts his beard, how much could it grow during his lifetime?

a. About 30 feet

b. About 55 feet

8 People **blink** to keep the eyeballs moist and clean with tears. People also blink if they are tired or to keep out bright lights. What we feel or think can also affect how much we blink. During a day, the average woman blinks

a. Twice as often as a man

b. Half as often as a man

9 What is the **hardest** part of the body?

a. The enamel in your teeth

b. The skull

10 About six quarts of blood are carried through the body by **blood vessels**. The vessels range in size from about an inch wide to capillaries (*cap*-ill-air-eez) too small to see with the naked eye. How many miles of blood vessels are there in the body?

a. About 3,500 miles. Stretched out, they'd go from New York City to London, England.

b. More than 93,000 miles. Stretched out, they'd circle Earth's equator nearly 4 times.

11 The 100 billion cells of the brain are called **neurons**. Neurons connect to each other by sending electrochemical signals. How fast do those signals move from neuron to neuron?

a. 250 miles per hour

b. 250 miles per second

12 The **heart** beats 100,000 times a day, sending blood through the body. How long does it take a single blood cell to travel completely through the body once?

a. One minute

b. Six hours

Answers: 1, a; 2, b; 3, b; 4, a; 5, a; 6, b; 7, a; 8, a; 9, a; 10, b; 11, a; 12, a.

Chapter 12
Incredible Mysteries

Today, we know why volcanoes erupt, what causes rainbows, and the answers to other mysteries that once puzzled humans. Yet science hasn't completely cleared up every mystery—at least not to the satisfaction of some. Have aliens landed on Earth? Were there ancient civilizations more advanced than ours? Maybe these mysteries will one day be solved…or maybe not.

In This Chapter

- A Giant or a Hoax?
- Invaders from Mars
- Mysterious Crop Circles

And Much More!

Incredible!

In 1912, a skull and jawbone were dug up in a pit in Piltdown, England. Scientists said they were from a creature—known as the Piltdown Man—who was the missing link between humans and apes. It turns out that the fossils were part human skull and part orangutan jaw. No one ever figured out who planted the fake bones. One of the main suspects was Sir Arthur Conan Doyle, the creator of Sherlock Holmes. The photo (right) a reconstruction of the infamous bones.

Incredible!

Some researchers claim crop circles are caused by electromagnetic radiation given off by the Earth. Visitors have sometimes said that their bodies tingle when near or in a circle.

Blast from the Past

A radio broadcast of the drama *War of the Worlds* was so scary to some people, they hid in cellars, fled in cars, loaded guns to defend themselves from Martians, and asked the power company to turn off the electricity so the Martians wouldn't see their town's lights.

"It is reported that at 8:50 P.M., a huge, flaming object, believed to be a meteorite, fell on a farm...."

The Hoax Hall of Fame

Hoaxes are tricks that fool people into believing completely made-up stories. Some hoaxers have fooled the world into believing the most outrageous lies. For these tricksters, every day is April Fool's Day.

The Giant Mystery Man

In 1869, while digging a well, a pair of farmers in Cardiff, New York, unearthed a **10-foot-tall, 3,000 pound fossilized man.** Many people, scientists among them, said that the huge human was a member of an ancient race of giants. Thousands of people lined up to see it. The truth was less mysterious: A hoaxer had a stonecutter carve the giant from a five-ton rock, then aged it, and paid the farmers to bury and find it. In 1947, the **Cardiff Giant** was sold to the Farmer's Museum in Cooperstown, New York. It is still on display there.

Incredible!

In 1912, bones were dug up in a pit in Piltdown, England. Scientists said that they were from the missing link between humans and apes. Not everyone believed the Piltdown Man was for real, but it took 40 years to prove it was a fake. It turns out the fossils were part human skull and part orangutan jaw.

Checkmate!

The Turk was no computer, but this chess-playing machine was able to beat almost all opponents for 84 years, from the late 1700s through the middle of the 1800s. The machine was a wooden figure placed on top of a table with mechanical arms to make moves. Under the table were drawers, which the Turk's owner opened to show its machinery. The secret? A series of human chess masters hid inside the Turk and made the moves. Although experts finally figured out the mystery, people kept playing against the Turk.

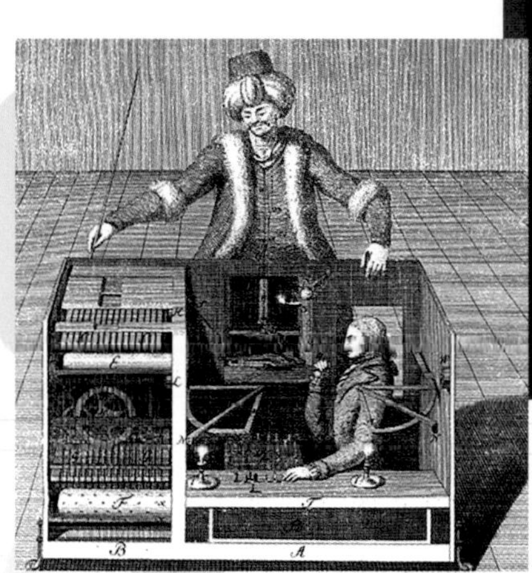

This drawing reveals the secret of the Turk: Hidden in the cabinet was a person who made the chess moves.

DAILY NEWS — NEW YORK'S PICTURE NEWSPAPER — FINAL

New York, Monday, October 31, 1938

FAKE RADIO 'WAR' STIRS TERROR THROUGH U.S.

Story on Page 2

"War" Victim

Caroline Cantlon, WPA actress, listening to this radio in West 49th St., heard announcement of "smoke in Times Square." Running to street, she fell, broke her arm.

"I Didn't Know".

The Martians Are Coming!

Listeners to the radio on Halloween in 1938 heard a series of frightening news bulletins. They reported that Earth was under attack by Martians. Many panicked listeners ran into the streets and called police and the newspapers. People later learned that the news flashes were part of a performance of the science fiction novel ***War of the Worlds***. The cast made the hoax sound real—too real.

BTW

In 1998, a monument to the *War of the Worlds* broadcast was placed in Van Nest Park, in Grover's Mill, New Jersey. That was the site where the Martian invaders supposedly landed.

Tales of the Unknown

Is there a lost city hidden in the rain forests of the Amazon? Why did the ancient Mayan civilization in Mexico disappear? Did an alien spaceship crash land and is it in a military base in Nevada? History is full of mysteries. Some of them can be explained, and some still keep us guessing about what is true and what is made up.

BTW

People who study crop circles are called cerealogists. The name comes from the Roman goddess of agriculture, Ceres. Another name for these people is croppies.

They Keep Cropping Up

Crop circles are mysterious patterns made in fields by flattening down wheat, corn, or other crops. Some of them are simple circles. Others are very complicated patterns. Crop circles started to appear in England in the 1960s and '70s. Then more and more circles and formations began to, well, crop up. Some people believe they were made when alien spacecraft landed. Or maybe they are some sort of message from visitors from space. A few scientists think the circles might be caused by spinning columns of air. Most people, however, believe they are pranks. A few hoaxers admitted they made some circles with a plank of wood attached to a rope. Still, some folks say that pranks can't be the only reason for the thousands of circles.

Strange Statues

Easter Island is part of Polynesia, a series of islands in the southeastern Pacific Ocean. When Europeans first landed on the island in the 1700s, they found a few thousand natives and 887 large stone statues. The figures were as tall as 14 feet and weighed many tons. No one knows for sure how or why they were built. There are many wild theories about the creators of the statues, including one that claims space aliens carved the stone figures. Experts say the statues were made by the island's original inhabitants.

Blast from the Past

Easter Island's native population was once about 12,000. By the time the Europeans arrived, their numbers had been reduced by natural disasters—and also because building and moving the statues used up the island's resources.

Do Monsters Exist?

Is there such a thing as a sea serpent? Do dinosaurs still walk the Earth? Is it possible that the Abominable Snowman is real? So far, no one has proven that these mysterious creatures exist. On the other hand, no one has proven they don't.

Incredible!

Cryptozoology (krip-toh-zoo-*ah*-loh-gee) is the study of hidden animals. Cryptozoologists are people who search for evidence that legendary creatures, such as Big Foot and the Loch Ness Monster, are real. They also hope to discover new and unusual animal species, such as giant bats.

Big Birds

A **teratorn** is an extinct flying bird that had a wingspan of 23 feet. Some people claim to have seen birds nearly as large flapping around parts of North America. Supposedly, a few of these extra-large birds are huge owls. Others are said to have bat-like wings. The name given to any of these big birds is thunderbirds. There are those who say thunderbirds have tried to carry off humans. Despite their size, no one has photographed these birds.

Yeti Another Monster

There are people who claim to have seen the **Yeti**, or Abominable Snowman, or at least its footprints. The creature is said to live in the snowy mountain regions of Nepal, India, and Tibet, countries in Asia. The Yeti has been described as six feet tall, covered in hair or fur, and having a pointed head. There are those who think a Yeti might be an unknown species of animal, such as a bear. Others believe it is a kind of gorilla. Still others say it doesn't exist except in people's imaginations.

BTW

In 1960, an expedition in search of the Yeti found this scalp in a monastery in Nepal. Was it from the Abominable Snowman? Some said the hairs came from a rare type of antelope. Others said the scalp was from a monkey-like creature. The scalp now sits in the monastery—and remains an unsolved mystery.

Monster alert! The photos taken of Champ are a little out of focus. Unfortunately, they are too blurry to clear up the mystery of the creature.

The Monster in the Lake

Lake Champlain stretches for 100 miles on the border of Vermont, New York, and the Canadian province of Quebec. For 400 years, people have reported that a creature lives in the lake. Nicknamed **Champ**, the animal is said to be between 20 and 40 feet long and to look like a dinosaur or serpent. Believers say a dinosaur got trapped in the lake millions of years ago and its offspring now live there. Others say Champ may be a kind of whale or other large marine animal. Whatever it is (or isn't), loads of tourists come to Vermont hoping to see Champ.

This photo of Champ was taken in 1977. Doubters say the picture shows a tree trunk or log sticking out of the water, and the "body" is just a shadow.

Blast from the Past

The legends of two Native American tribes living in the Lake Champlain area mention a lake monster. The first sighting of Champ came in 1883. A local sheriff claimed to have seen a water serpent near the shore of Lake Champlain.

Chapter 13 Incredible Constructions

From ancient pyramids to modern skyscrapers, architects and engineers have been dazzling us with their designs for centuries. Today's constructions are more astonishing than ever before. Bridges are longer and more unusual looking, buildings are taller and constructed in weird shapes–and gardens are being grown sideways!

In This Chapter

- Gardens on the Sides of Buildings
- A Bridge that Curls Up
- Get Lost in a Maze

And Much More!

Blast from the Past

In 1968, it was decided to scrape off the original paint on the Golden Gate Bridge in San Francisco, California, and repaint it. It took 27 years to finish the job.

BTW

This living wall is made of grass. It's growing on the side of a building in Santiago, Chile. An irrigation system behind the vertical garden delivers water containing plant nutrients. The grass doesn't need soil to grow.

BTW

This is the plan of a garden in Barcelona, Spain. Is it a labyrinth or a maze? If you said maze, you're right. Find out why on page 178.

These Walls Are Alive!

One way to make a city green is to grow plants on the roofs of buildings. Another is to grow plants on the sides of buildings. Known as living walls or vertical gardens, they are sprouting everywhere, including museums, office buildings, and airports. Living works of art, they bring a touch of nature to city streets.

Green Thumb

The largest garden wall in North America is in **Longwood Gardens**, in Kennett Square, Pennsylvania. The living wall includes more than 47,000 plants, most of them ferns. The plants reduce air pollution and cut down on noise.

Chile's Cool Garden

One of the largest vertical gardens in the world is on two sides of a 16-story hotel in Santiago, Chile. The plants were placed in **4,300 separate panels**, each two feet by two feet. They cover an area that is about the size of six tennis courts.

BTW

Vertical gardens shade a building in the summer and insulate the building in winter, keeping in warmth.

Wall of Fame

Patrick Blanc created the first vertical garden in 1988. The botanist, a scientist who studies plants, went on to make this vertical garden on the outside of a museum in Paris, France. The plants are held in place by cloth attached to metal frames, or panels.

An irrigation system behind the green wall delivers water containing plant nutrients. The plants don't need soil to grow.

BTW

Green walls are expensive to keep up. Since rain doesn't fall sideways, the plants need constant irrigation and electronic monitoring to make sure they get enough water. But irrigating with recycled water and putting in plants native to an area can help cut down on the use of resources.

musée du quai Branly

musée des arts et civilisations d'Afrique, d'Asie, d'Océanie et des Amériques

entrée Branly

Those Wild and Crazy Buildings

Sometimes architects like to think outside the box. New technology has allowed them to build structures in all kinds of shapes and materials. The buildings can make passersby do a double take.

The Experience of a Lifetime

This building rocks! **The Experience Music Project** is a museum in Seattle, Washington, that's devoted to the history of rock 'n' roll. It's also home to the Science Fiction Museum and Hall of Fame. The building's wild curves are the brainchild of world-famous architect Frank Gehry. One architecture critic says the building looks like it crawled out of the sea, rolled over, and died!

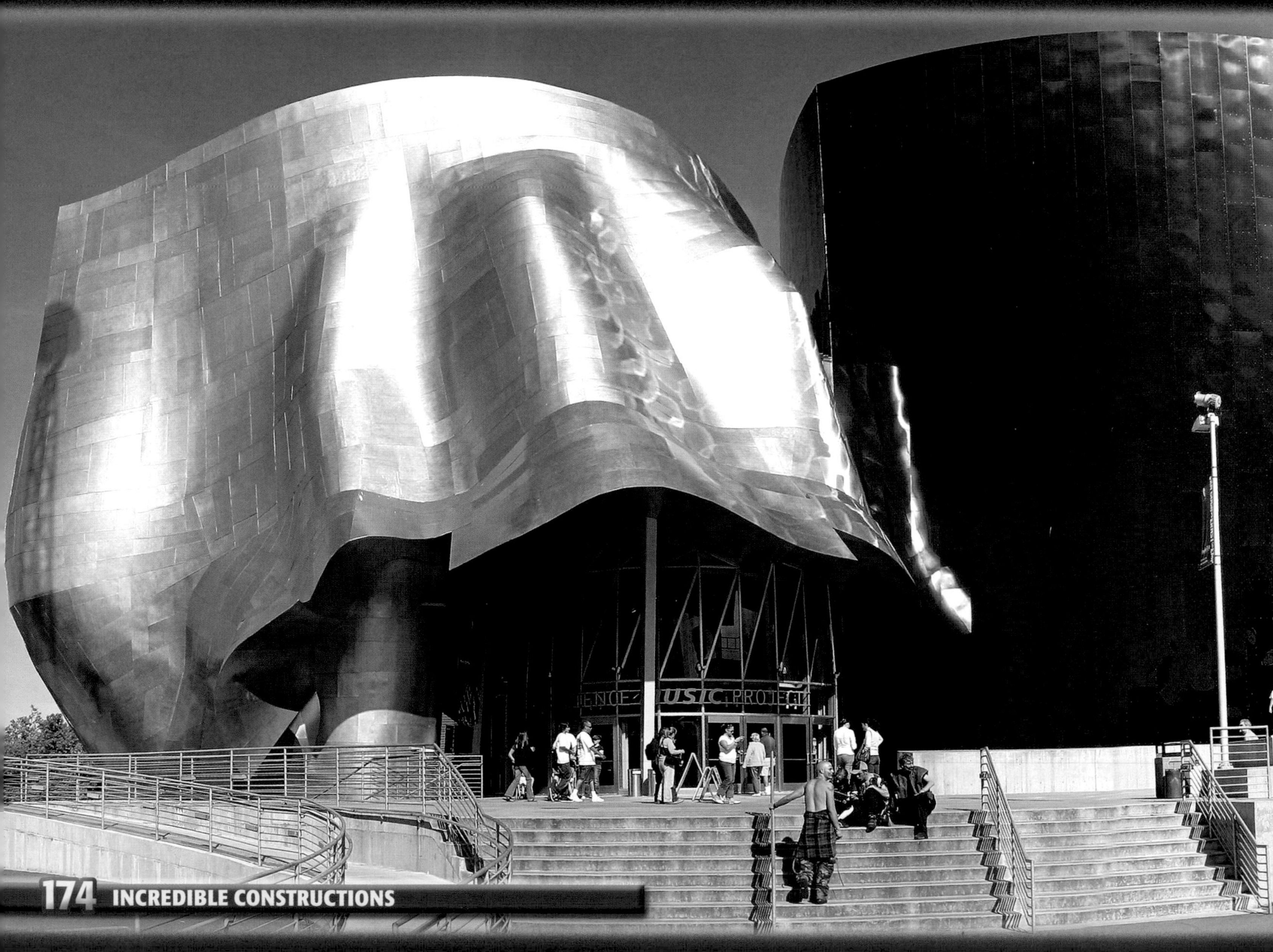

Check This Out

You can't stuff these library books into a backpack! This **wall of books** was built next to the Kansas City Public Library, in Kansas City, Missouri. There are 22 books represented, and each spine is about 25 feet high and nine feet wide. The titles, suggested by Kansas City readers, include *Lord of the Rings*, *Charlotte's Web*, *The Adventures of Huckleberry Finn*, *To Kill a Mockingbird*, and *Silent Spring*.

For the Record

The largest library in the world is the Library of Congress, in Washington, D.C. It has more than 33 million books and other print materials. The shelves holding all its items would reach 838 miles.

Making Waves

It looks like something out of a fairy tale—on purpose. The architect was inspired by a Polish artist who illustrated fairy-tale books. The **Crooked House**, located in Sopot, Poland, really casts a spell on you. Even the shingles on the roof look like dragon scales.

Bodacious Bridges

A bridge has a simple job: to allow people and vehicles to cross an obstacle, such as a river. But every obstacle is different, and so are bridges. Some are stone, some are steel. Some are shaped like arches, others are supported by cables. Some bridges cross a valley, others cross a sea. Some bridges are ordinary looking, and some are one-of-a-kind.

Wave Hello!

No vehicles cross the Henderson Waves bridge. It's a good thing, because it might make drivers dizzy. This pedestrian bridge in Singapore, a nation in Asia, looks like a huge snake. Built above a park, the bridge has steel ribs that seem to flow above and below a wooden deck in wonderful waves.

Curl Up with a Good Bridge

The Rolling Bridge in London, England, seems pretty ordinary. The 36-foot-long metal bridge lets people pass from one side of a walkway to another. But when it lets a boat pass through it, the bridge does something amazing: One end rises up and curls back onto its other end, forming a circle. After the boat has passed, the bridge uncurls itself.

High, There!

The highest bridge for vehicles is the Millau Viaduct in France, which spans the valley of the Tarn River. At its highest point, the bridge is 1,125 feet above the valley floor, higher than the Eiffel Tower.

Usually the Millau Viaduct is only open to cars. But here, about 10,000 runners cross the bridge during a 14-mile-long race.

1,125 ft high

For the Record

The world's longest bridge over water is the Quingdao Haiwan Bridge. At 26.4 miles long, it crosses Jiaozhou Bay, in eastern China. The bridge is held up by 5,200 columns.

A-Maze-ing Mazes

There are mazes you solve with a pencil and then there are mazes you solve with your legs. Walk-through mazes are an incredible experience. These large-scale mazes are made of such materials as hedges, turf, paving stones, bricks, and even sand. Some are so big, with walls so tall, people can get lost in them. Some are permanent, and some wash away at high tide.

A Maze with a View

It's easy to lose your way in **Longleat's hedge maze.** Located in England, it has about 1¾ miles of paths walled in by more than 16,000 tall English yews (a kind of hedge). There are six bridges throughout the maze. Maze-goers climb them to get a view of their goal at the center of the maze: an observation tower.

BTW

The Longleat maze covers 1.48 acres. Depending on how good you are at solving it, it might take you from 20 to 90 minutes to reach its center.

BTW

A **maze** has many pathways: Some will lead to the goal while others are dead ends. A **labyrinth** has only one pathway that leads from the entrance to the goal—although the pathway can be long and winding.

A Sand Blast

A beach is the perfect place to create a **sand labyrinth**. This one was made in California by an artist named Kirkos, using a roller on wet sand. It is a copy of a famous stone labyrinth laid onto the floor of Chartres Cathedral, near Paris, France. The 800-year-old **Chartres labyrinth** is still around.

Chapter 14 Incredible Micro Worlds

On us, in us, and around us are life forms so tiny that you can't see them with the naked eye. And now humans are creating objects as small or smaller than the littlest living things. Called nanomaterials, they can only be seen with special electron microscopes. They might one day be used to create micro robots, super-fast computer circuits, or tools to treat disease.

Incredible!

A **nanoparticle** with a diameter of four nanometers is one million times smaller than an ant. A **nanotube** with a diameter of one nanometer is 100,000 times thinner than a strand of hair.

In This Chapter

- Meet the Teeny Beetles
- Mighty Small Mites
- The Weird World of Nanoparticles

And Much More!

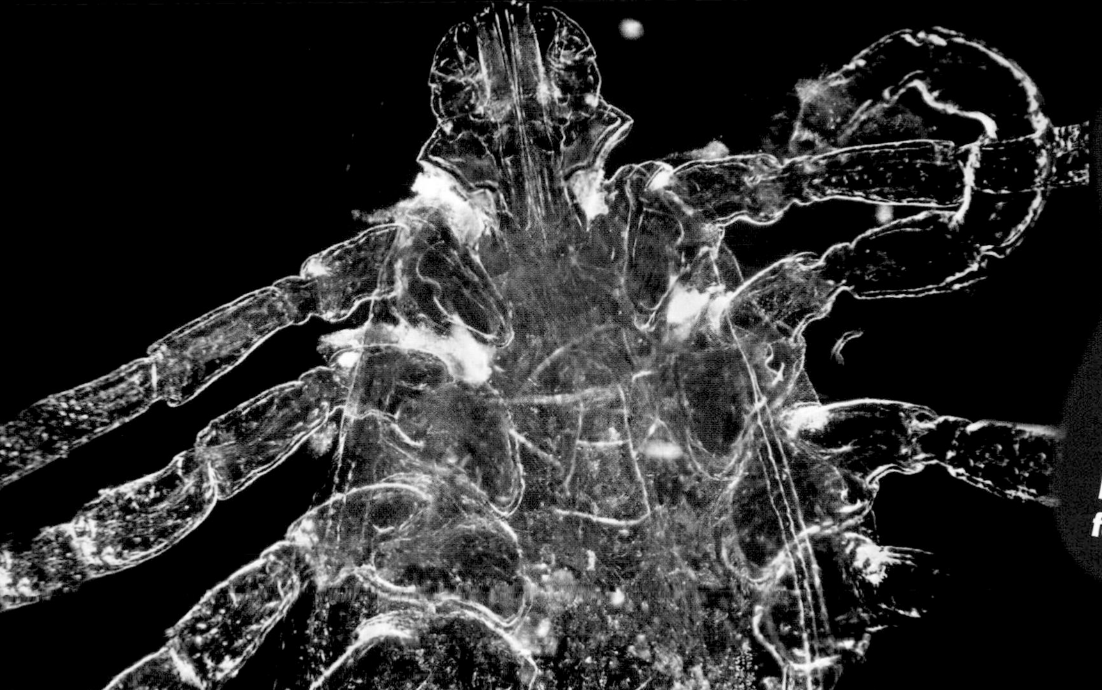

Incredible!

Mites are invisible creatures that live in some people's eyelashes, but not in the millions of other hairs that cover the human body. Most of these hairs are too thin to see. Only the lips, palms of the hands, and the soles of the feet have no hair.

BTW

The woodboring beetle is a very small beetle that lays its eggs in furniture and other wooden objects. When the egg hatches, a larva comes out. A larva is the early stage of a beetle before it becomes an adult. The larva eats its way out of the wood, leaving behind a tiny hole and some sawdust.

Nano Wonders

When scientists want to measure very small objects, the scale they use is the nanometer. A nanometer is one-billionth of a meter. (A meter is about 3.3 feet.) A sheet of paper is about 100,000 nanometers thick. Objects in the natural world, such as sea spray and proteins in our bodies, are nano-sized. Scientists are also creating objects that are between one and 100 nanometers in size. These nanomaterials include tiny particles and tubes, and ultra-thin sheets. Scientists hope to learn more about these materials and how they can be used in computers, medicine, and other areas. The only way to see objects on the nanoscale is with special, powerful microscopes. Viewed close up, nano-size objects look strange and unearthly.

Flower Power

You're not looking at a bunch of flowers. You're looking at tiny nanomaterials—each a quarter of the size of a droplet of fog. A special light makes them glow green. (The pink was added to the photo.) This technology could be used to study human cells or to send drugs to exact areas in the body.

Incredible!

Your fingernail grows at a rate of one nanometer per second.

Have a Nano Ball!

It looks like lots of little fingers holding a pink ball. But the "fingers" are **nano-bristles**, and they are hundreds of times thinner than a human hair. (The image was digitally colored to give the nano-bristles pink fingernails.) They were put in liquid, and when the liquid evaporated, the bristles twisted themselves around the round object. The possible uses of nano-bristles include delivering drugs to the body and in materials that clean themselves.

Mini Melons

A patch of melons? No, these **nano-orbs** were shaped by magnets operating on tiny iron particles in liquid. A special light hardened the melons. The now-magnetic balls might one day be used in color displays for computers and for delivering drugs to specific areas of the body.

BTW

There are many current uses of nanomaterials, from making lightweight sports equipment to coating the surface of eyeglasses and computer screens to make them easy to clean and harder to scratch.

Buggin' Out

Even if you're the only person at home, you've got company. There may be tiny creatures in your bed, your carpets, and in your kitchen cabinets–and possibly in your eyelashes. These unasked for roommates are arachnids (eight-legged creatures) and insects. They may look scary when magnified hundreds of times, but don't worry–every home has them, they're invisible, and they're harmless.

Mighty Mite

What's hanging out in your bed? Millions of **dust mites**. These harmless, microscopic bugs live in mattresses, pillows, and carpets. Their favorite food is flakes of dead skin that rub off our bodies.

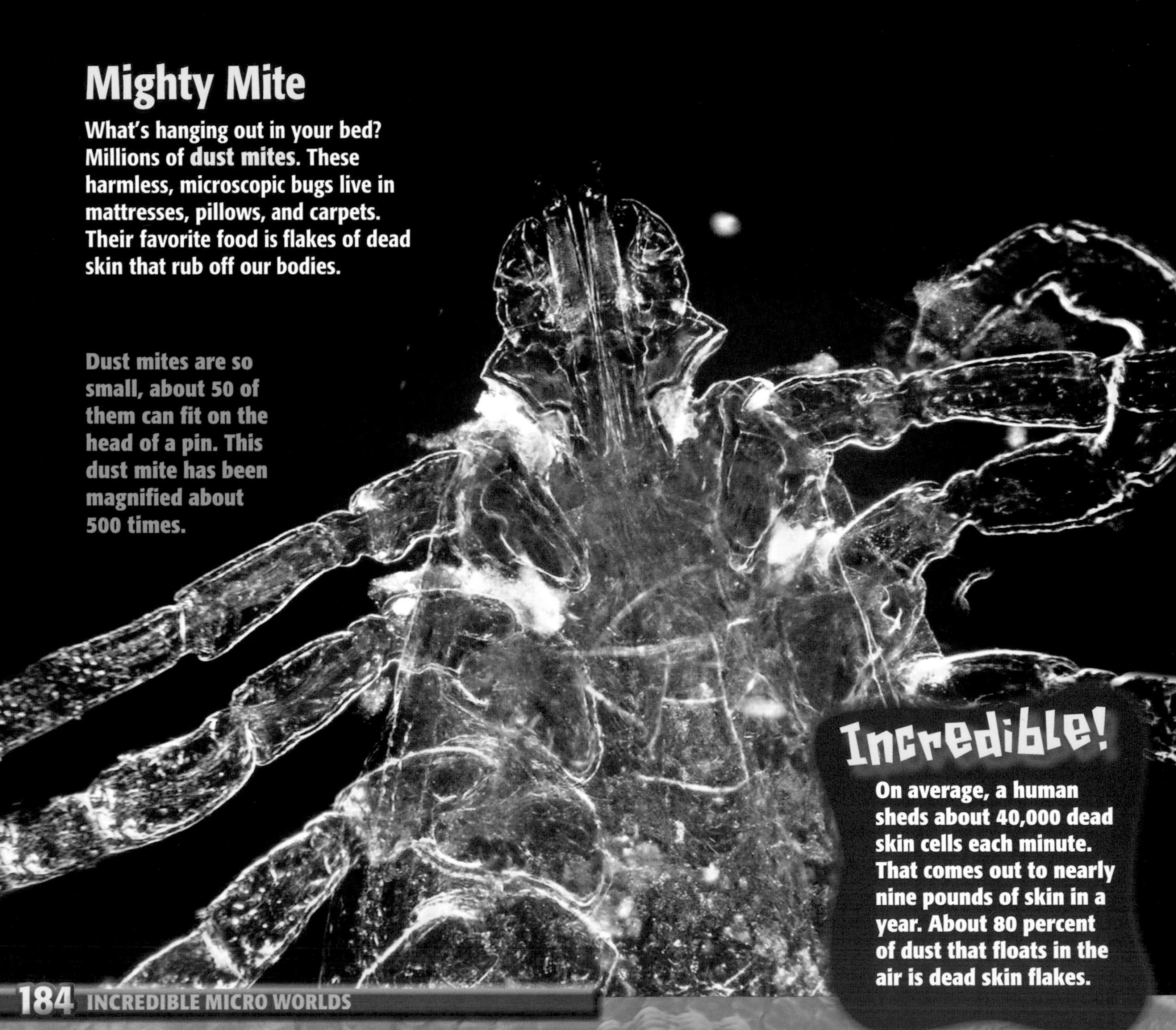

Dust mites are so small, about 50 of them can fit on the head of a pin. This dust mite has been magnified about 500 times.

Incredible!

On average, a human sheds about 40,000 dead skin cells each minute. That comes out to nearly nine pounds of skin in a year. About 80 percent of dust that floats in the air is dead skin flakes.

Evil Weevil

Beetles are usually pretty large. Not the weevil. This beetle is often no bigger than a grain of rice—which is what some weevils love to eat. The **rice weevil's** powerful little jaws chew a hole into the kernel of rice, then it lays eggs inside. Weevils snack on other foods, such as nuts, beans, seeds, and grains. A flour beetle eats just about anything, from crackers and pasta to peas and chocolate. Sealing these foods in airtight containers is one way to keep weevils from holding a feast in your kitchen.

Incredible!

Millions of hairs cover the human body. Most are too thin to see. Only the lips, palms of the hands, and the soles of the feet have no hair.

Do you know what you are looking at? (The answer is upside down below.)

What an Eyeful

Don't look now, but your eyelashes might be a home for mites. Called follicle mites or **eyelash mites**, these microscopic creatures sometimes can live in some people's eyelash follicles (the tiny openings hair grows out of). Though the thought of these invisible mites sounds gross, they're totally harmless and people don't even know they are there.

Answer: human nose hair

Chapter 15

Incredible Kids

There are more than 41 million people between the ages of 5 and 14 in the United States. Many of these young people are helping others, breaking ground in sports and entertainment, working to improve the environment, and being creative in many fields. Check out some kids who have made a difference.

In This Chapter

- A 10-Year-Old Girl Discovers an Exploding Star
- This Kid Climbed Mount Everest
- She's a Baseball Whiz Kid
- The Boy Who Is the Doodle King

And Much More!

Incredible!

Jordan Romero climbed Mount Everest at age 13. He is the youngest of the almost 3,000 people who have reached the summit.

Incredible!

When Jessica Watson was 16, she sailed nonstop around the world by herself. She traveled 23,000 miles over seven months on a 34-foot boat. During her voyage, Jessica ran into fierce storms and giant waves. She is thought to be the youngest person ever to sail solo around the world. Jessica hopes her feat will inspire other young people to challenge themselves.

Kids Conquer the World

Kids through the ages have performed remarkable feats. The great composer Wolfgang Amadeus Mozart wrote a symphony when he was 9. King Tutankhamen was a teenager when he ruled as pharaoh of Egypt. And today's kids are also making their marks on the world.

A Super Discovery

At age 10, Kathryn Gray, of Fredericton, New Brunswick, in Canada, became the youngest person to discover a supernova, or exploding star. With the help of her dad and special computer software, she found a supernova galaxy 240 million light-years away. Kathryn hopes to make more such discoveries in the future.

The Doodle King

Drawing doodles is serious business for Lim Ding Wen. When he was 9, he created a program called *Doodle Kids*. Users draw pictures with their fingers directly onto the screen of the Apple iPhone and shake the phone to clear the screen. At age 10, he created *Invader War*, a space arcade game also for the iPhone. Lim, who lives in Singapore, in Southeast Asia, has created about 20 computer programs.

Peak Experience

At age 13, **Jordan Romero**, of Big Bear, California, had a goal to climb Mt. Everest, the tallest mountain in the world. He set out on that adventure with his father and several guides. Jordan overcame difficulties on the climb to become the youngest person to reach the summit of Everest. Currently Jordan plans on climbing the tallest mountain in each of the 50 states.

Kids Make a Big Difference

Kid power can achieve a lot. Young people are helping others in need and accomplishing great things in areas such as sports, the environment, and fashion. These kids serve as role models for other kids—and adults!

Warm Heart, Warm Feet

Hannah Turner wants to make sure that no one in her Ohio community gets cold feet. She and her family run a charity called Hannah's Socks. The organization collects new socks and gives them to the homeless. It started when Hannah was 4 years old and worked at a local shelter for homeless people. She noticed a man with ripped shoes that revealed bare toes. She made up her mind to help. So far, Hannah's Socks has collected more than 21,000 pairs of socks. Her goal: 200,000 pairs.

Fashion Sense

When she was 6, **Cecilia Cassini** asked for a sewing machine. Since then, her passion for fashion has turned into a career as a designer. By the time she was 12, she was making 25 to 30 dresses each week. Cecilia uses the Internet to sell her creations, and her clothes are also sold in some California stores. Cecilia's dream is to sell her designs in shops around the world.

She's Got Game

Strike three! You're out! Batters who go up against pitcher **Chelsea Baker** hear those words a lot. Chelsea pitches in an all-boys' league in Plant City, Florida. The young player hadn't lost a single Little League game in four years. In one season, she pitched two perfect games. At age 13, she became the youngest player to be honored by the National Baseball Hall of Fame, in Cooperstown, New York. One of her uniforms is on display in the Hall. Chelsea hopes to one day play professional ball.

Incredible!

The group Kids vs Global Warming wrote *The Declaration of Independence from Fossil Fuels*. It lets leaders know that young people want the U.S. to end its dependence on gas and oil. Nearly 50,000 kids have signed it so far.

An Eco Leader

Alec Loorz wants to put a freeze on global warming. When he was 12 years old, the California teen founded Kids vs Global Warming. The nonprofit group teaches young people about climate change and what they can do to stop it. One way to fight global warming is by planting trees, which Alec likes to do (as shown in the photo). Alec has given more than 150 talks on climate to audiences. He is inspiring other kids to speak out on the issue, which will affect young people more than anyone.

Chapter 16

Incredibly Weird but True

In this book you've read some incredible facts and seen some incredible photos. But in this chapter, you're going to experience the world of the weird. Don't be nervous: The people, places, and things you will meet aren't scary. They're just...weird.

In This Chapter

- Naturally Preserved Mummies
- A See-Through Frog
- T-Shirts Made of Leaves

And Much More!

Incredible!

The tiny Museum of the Weird in Austin, Texas, has weird objects from all over—including a three-eyed cow and a Cabinet of Curiosities—all of which are very weird indeed!

BTW

Artist Dave Rittinger has created a series of shirts made out of real leaves. Rittinger collects the leaves from trees at a park and glues them together. The shirts come in leaves of summer green, autumn colors, and winter brown. They're guaranteed to "leaf" you astonished!

What's so special about this frog? Turn to page 196 to find out.

Blast from the Past

When most people think of mummies, they think of Egypt. But recently, some mummies were discovered in China. The Chinese mummies weren't created by people—they were created by nature thousands of years ago.

Now That's Weird!

The world is full of odd, peculiar, unusual, out-of-the-ordinary, and downright weird people, places, and things. Of course, weird can also be wonderful.

Turning Over a New Leaf

For artist **Dave Rittinger**, autumn is the best season. That's when he can gather up the raw materials for the T-shirts he makes: leaves. Rittinger puts together the leaves by hand and glues them in place. They may be a little prickly and hard to clean. But when it's time to throw away one of these T-shirts, you can simply toss it outside and let nature turn it into mulch.

Now Hair This!

Bigger—and odder—is always better at the **International Fantasy Hair Competition**. Every year, contestants create some unusual hairdos. But that isn't the end of it. On top of their hair, contestants place sculptures, including castles, pirate ships, and the Eiffel Tower. This contestant's hair is shaped into a peacock to go along with a headful of fake feathers. It's hair raising!

Scorpion Suckers

The **Bone Room** in Berkeley, California, is the place to shop if you're looking to buy human and animal skulls, skeletons, fossils, framed insects, and other items that were once alive. If you have a taste for the weird, try snacking on the store's chocolate-covered crickets, cookie wafers mixed with ants, or lollipops with real scorpions in the center!

Now That's Weirder!

One thing you can always count on: Weird stuff happens every day. The steady stream of the unexpected and unusual never fails to astonish us.

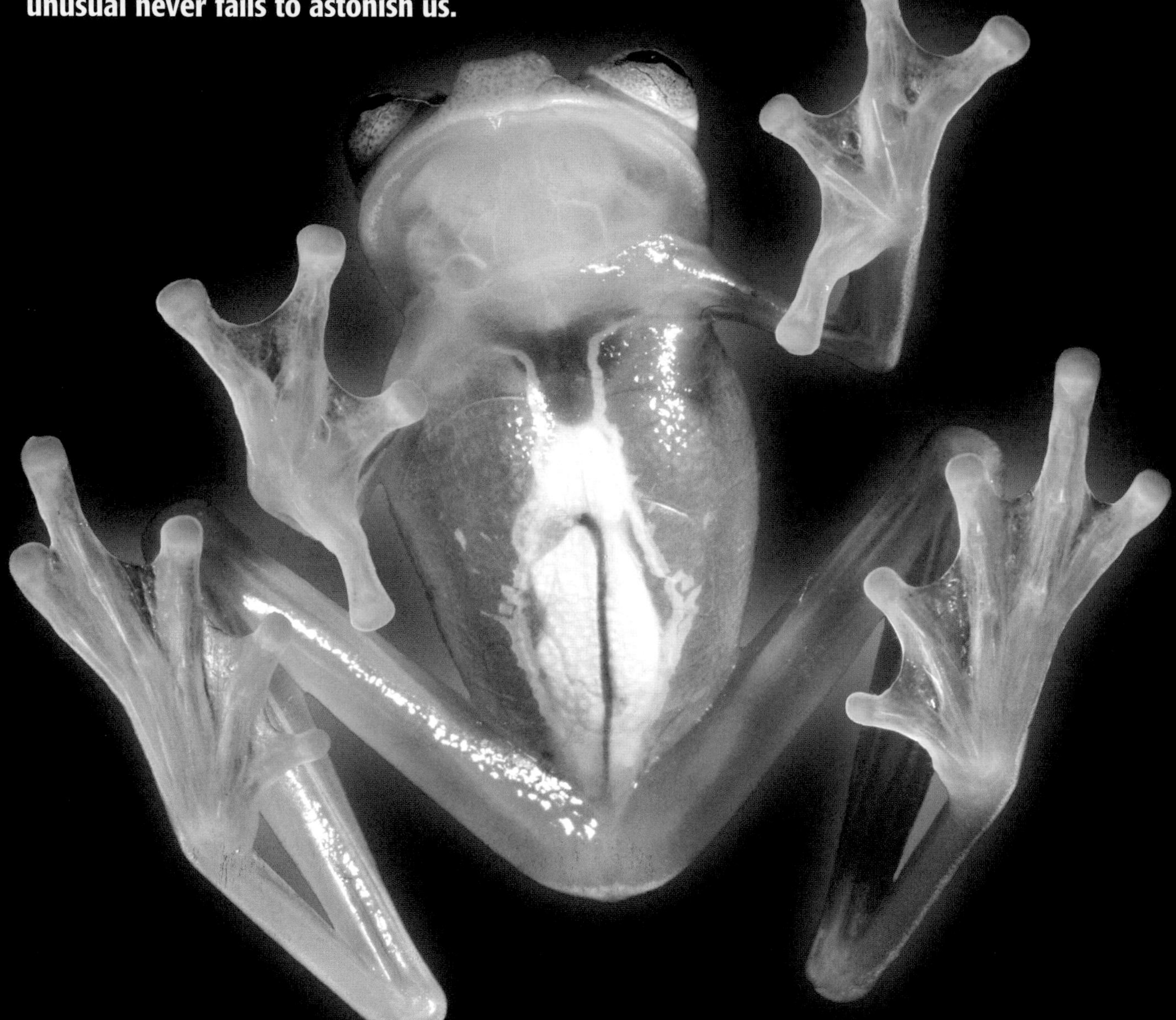

The Inner Frog

The glass frog of Central and South America is a show off. Its transparent skin lets you see its internal organs. The frog's beating heart, liver, and digestive system are visible from its underside. Viewed from its top side, the frog appears to be a normal shade of green or brown. But a closer look reveals the frog's bones beneath its skin. Why the frog has see-through skin remains a mystery to scientists.

It Can Bear the Heat

The **water bear** is one of the weirdest animals on Earth. The tiny creature can't be seen with the naked eye. It has eight legs, lives almost everywhere, and got its name because it is said to walk like a bear. But what makes it odd is that almost nothing can kill it. Water bears can live in temperatures as cold as -459°F, which is close to absolute zero (the coldest temperature in the universe). Temperatures as high as 304°F don't kill it, nor does a dose of radiation that would kill just about any other animal. The hardy animal can live almost 10 years without water.

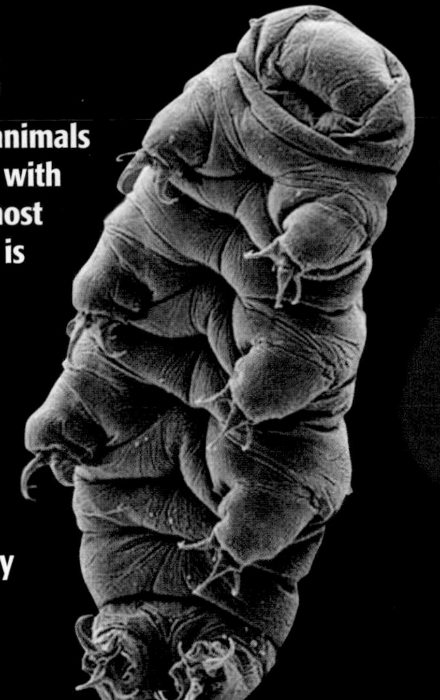

Incredible!

Astronauts took a few water bears into orbit and left them out for 10 days in airless space. Most of them survived!

Mysterious Mummies

This **mummy** isn't an ancient Egyptian pharaoh. It's from China, where it was buried under desert sands for 3,500 years. The body was perfectly preserved by the region's dry weather and the natural salts in the ground. Even the woman's brown hair and eyelashes survived the centuries. This and other mummies traveled to several U.S. museums before returning to China.

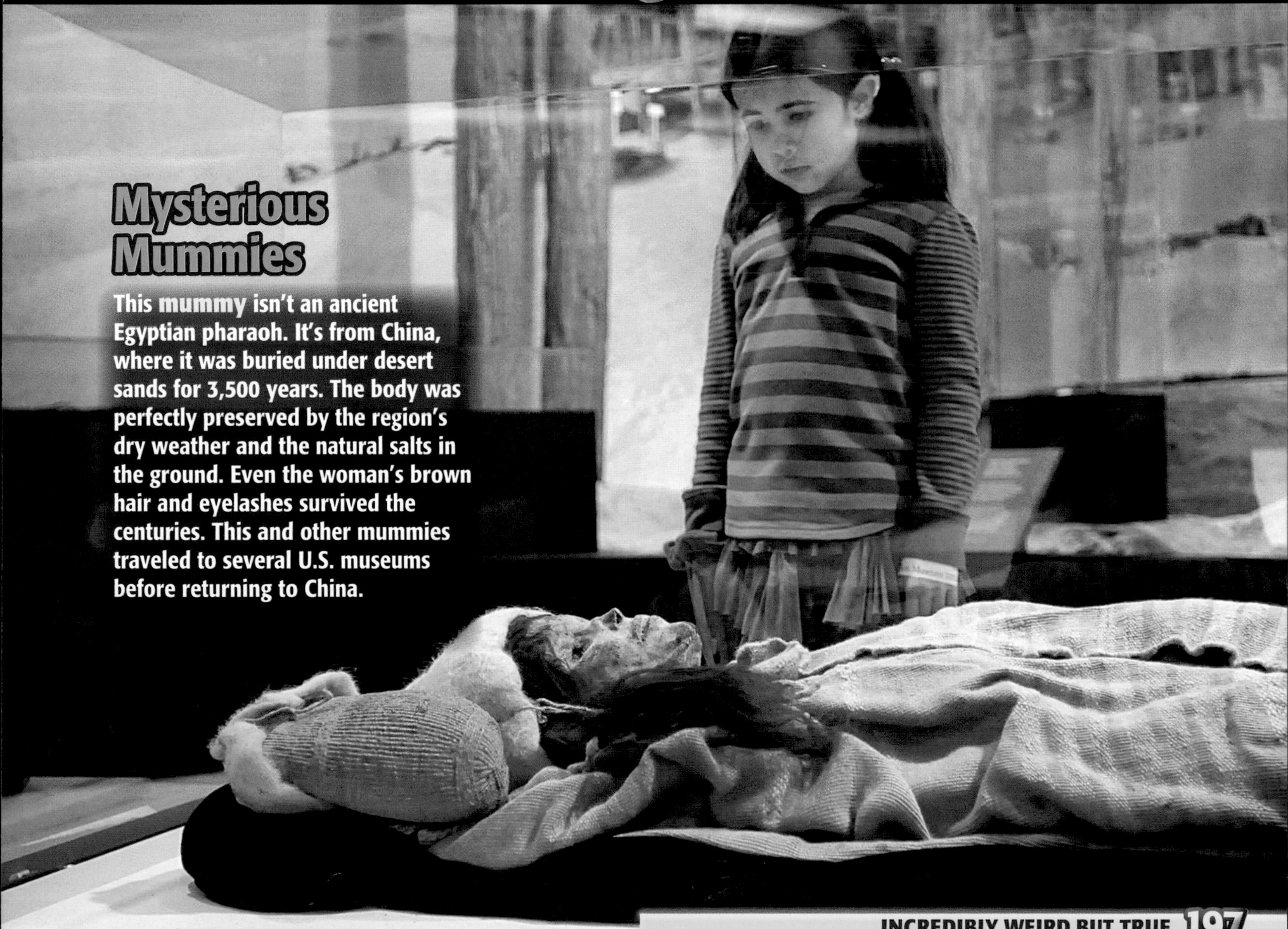

Where in the World?

The world is full of surprises. Below are some incredible facts about some places across the globe. Can you match each fact to its location on the map? The answers are printed upside down below.

Incredible Facts

1. It's the only land on Earth not owned by any country.

2. This is the only city located on two continents.

3. There are about 2 million lakes in this country—more than in any other nation.

4. At just 8.1 square miles, it's the smallest island in the world that's also a nation.

5. The deepest hole ever dug by humans—more than seven miles down—is in this country.

6. This is the only South American country that touches both the Caribbean Sea and the Pacific Ocean.

7. This is the only country in the Middle East that has no desert.

8. In the U.S., coffee grows only in this state.

9. Of all the continents, only this one has kangaroos.

10. More than half of the U.S. coastline is in this state.

11. It's the only country with a flag that isn't a square or a rectangle. Instead, it's shaped like triangles.

12. At 2,700 miles, it's the longest country in world.

13. This nation is made up of more than 17,000 islands, the largest string of islands in the world.

14. Only three nations are surrounded completely by another nation. San Marino and the Vatican are surrounded by Italy. This is the other country.

15. This city's ceremonial full name is 163 letters, the longest place name in the world: Krung thep maha nakorn amorn ratana kosinmahintar ayutthay amaha dilok phop noppa ratrajathani burirom udom rajaniwesmahasat harn amorn phimarn avatarn sathit sakkattiya visanukamprasit.

Answer: 1. I, 2. G, 3. A, 4. M, 5. J, 6. B, 7. F, 8. D, 9. O, 10. E, 11. K, 12. C, 13. N, 14. H, 15. L

Index

A

Acton, Patrick, 122, 129
Africa, 51, 104
Afro-American Cultural Center, 131
Airbus A380, 144-145
AirPod car, 141
airsickness bags, 124
Alamaden Tower, 149
Alaska, 58
Alexiev, Ryan, 92
Allure of the Seas, 15
American curl cat, 47
Andes mountains, 104
animals
    as pets for pro athletes, 76-77
    camouflage, 48-49
    communication skills, 54-55
    hybrid, 50-51
    in Chinese Zodiac, 87
    life span, 40-41
    migrations, 58
Antarctica, 57, 58, 104, 105
appendix, 159
Apple iPhone, 188
aquatic brown frog, 61
Arado weeHouse, 31
Arches National Park, 95
Arctic Ocean, 58
Arctic tern, 59
Argentina, 104
Arizona, 115
Arlington, MA, 125
art
    carved crayons, 87
    Dalton Ghetti's pencil alphabet, 25
    food used in, 84-85
    Leshan Giant Buddha, 24
    portraits, 92-93
    self-portraits, 86, 93
    sepia ink used by artists, 48
    unusual materials, 84-85, 92-93
Asanuma, Mariann, 131
Asia, 51, 104, 176
Aspen, CO, 78
Austin, TX, 127, 192
Australia, 33, 35, 39, 59, 104, 105, 110, 116

B

Babe Ruth, 65
bacteria
    as the longest-lived life-form, 41
    in Komodo dragon's saliva, 42
Bagger 288, 16
Baja California, 58
Baker, Chelsea, 191
Baltimore Orioles, 65
Bank of America Tower, 149
barren-ground caribou, 59
Beijing, China, 82
Berkeley, CA, 125, 195
bicycles
    bendable, 142
    in the Netherlands, 142
    Tour de France, 143
    VW bik.e, 143
    Xylon, 143
Big Bear, CA, 189
Bigfoot, 127
bike polo, 69
Blaine, David, 131, 133
Blanc, Patrick, 173
blinking, 161
blood
    animal and human, 36-37
    tick body filled with human, 36
blood vessels
    capillaries, 155
    in the human body, 161
BMW, 82
Body Worlds
    Gunther von Hagens, 154
    human arm and hand, 155
    human head, 154
    Plastination, 154
    skeletal muscles in soccer player, 155
bog snorkeling, 71
Bohdran, Michael, 128
Bonds, Barry, 65
Bone Room, The, 125, 195
bonobos, 55
Borneo, 61
Boston Red Sox, 73
bottlenose dolphin, 50
bowhead whale, 40
brain
    neurons in, 161
    weight of, 160
Brazil, 33, 148
bread used as art, 84
Breakfast of Champions, 92
bridges
    Golden Gate, 170
    Henderson Waves, 176
    Rolling, 176
    Millian Viaduct, 177
    Quingdao Haiwan, 177
bristlecone pine, 40
British Crown Jewels, 102
bubbles, 18-19
bubble gum, 19
Buckner, Bill, 73
Buffalo Sabres, 66
Busti, Steve, 127, 192
butterflies
    monarch, 58
    owl, 44
Buttermilk Mountain, 78

C

Cabinet of Curiosities, 192
caldera, 115
California, 40, 47, 58, 96, 131, 189
Canada, 58, 67
Cape Canaveral, FL, 17
capybara, 20
carats, 102-103
Star of Africa, 102
Cardiff Giant, 164
Carlsbad, CA, 131
Carlsbad, NM, 41
Carter, Jimmy, 27
cassette tape, 93
Cassini spacecraft, 115
Cassini, Cecilia, 190
cassowary, 39
Castillo, Luis, 74
cats, 46-47
Cave of Crystals, 109
caves
    crystals in, 109
    Grotte Casteret, 108
    Krubera Cave, 135
    Ruby Falls, 108
    supercaves, 135
    underground, 108-109
caviar, 85
centaur, 51
Central America, 37, 48, 49
cerealogists, 166
Champ, 169
Charlotte, NC, 131
Chartres Cathedral, 179
Chattanooga, TN, 108

Chau, Diem, 87
Chicago Cubs, 74
Chicago, IL, 29
China, 81, 89, 144, 149, 177, 193, 197
Chinese Zodiac, 87
chocolate
  BMW, 82
  cave, 83
  chocolate-covered insects, 195
  Great Wall of China, 83
  in China, as medicine, 81
  terra cotta army, 82
  World Chocolate Dream Park, 82
Christmas Island, 59
Chronicles of Narnia, 89
Cincinnati Reds, 75
Cle Elum, WA, 77
Cleveland Indians, 75
Cockroach Hall of Fame, 128
cockroaches, 128
collisions
  of galaxies, 113
  of satellites, 120
  of stars, 112, 113
Colombia, 33
colossal squid, 11
Columbus, OH, 67
Connecticut, 100
Conwy, Wales, 30
Copacabana beach, 88
corpse flower, 32, 53
crab,
  red, 59
  yeti, 35
craters
  impact, 116-117
  in space, 114-115
crayons, 87
Crooked House, 175
crop circles
  cerealogists, 166
  how they are formed, 166
cryptozoology, 168
crystals, 109
cuttlefish, 48

D

Dead Sea, 99
Deep Green kite, 140
Delicate Arch, 95
Democratic Republic of the Congo, 33
Deneen, Patrick, 77
Denmark, 98
Des Moines, IA, 55
dhiru, 59
diamonds, 102-103
dinosaurs
  oviraptor fossil, 125
  Predator X, 12-13
  psittacosaur, 12
  raptorex, 13
  T. rex, 12-13
  trapped in Lake Champlain, 169
dogs
  ear protector for, 146
  how smart is your dog? 54
dolphins
  bottlenose, 50
  communication with, 54
  wholphins, 50
Doodle Kids, 188
Dorfman, Margaret, 81
double stars, 112
Doyle, Sir Arthur Conan, 162
Dunhuang Mogao Grottoes, 83
Dupont Jr., Ronald, 124

E

Earth
  asteroid impact, 116
  axis shift, 97
  crust, 96-97
  hit by meteorites, 116
  plates, 96-97
  seen from space, 100-101
  size comparison with sun, 119
  space trash orbiting, 120-121
  under attack by Martians, 165
  urban expansion, 101
earthquakes, 97
Easter Island, 167
Ecuador, 33
Egypt, 25, 193, 197
eLEGS, 157
EMILY (robotic buoy), 141
emperor penguin, 57
Empire State Building Run-up, 70
Empire State Building, 70
Enceladus, 111, 115
England, 65, 166, 176
erosion
  meaning of word, 107
  shaping rocks, 106-107
Europe, 104, 105
European sturgeon, 41
Experience Music Project, 174
eyelash
  as protector, 159
  mites, 185
EyeWriter, 153

F

false killer whale, 50
fangs, 34, 37
Farmer's Museum, Cooperstown, NY, 164
fingernails, 160, 182
Florida Marlins, 74
Florida, 51
flying frog, 59
food
  burnt, as collectible, 125
  used in art, 84-85
France, 132, 133, 143, 177
Frankenstein, 85
Fredericton, New Brunswick, Canada, 188
frilled lizard, 45
frogs
  aquatic brown, 61
  flying, 60
  glass, 193, 196
  goliath, 61
  Macaya breast-spot, 61
  vampire flying, 34

G

Galarraga, Armando, 75
galaxies
  Andromeda, 113
  colliding, 113
  definition, 113
  how many in the universe, 112
  largest diamond in, 102
  Milky Way, 19
  supernova, discovered by kid, 188
gems, 102-103
gemstones, 102
Georgetown, TX, 120
geysers
  on Earth, 115
  on Enceladus, 115
Ghetti, Dalton, 25
giant clam, 21
giant squid, 10-11
giant water bug, 8, 20
Gilbert, Alfred, 138
Gladrock, IA, 129
glass frog, 196

global warming, kids fighting, 191
goliath frog, 61
goliath tarantula, 20
Goreme Valley, 107
gray whales, 58
Gray, Kathryn, 188
Great Britain, 30
Great Chocolate Wall, 83
Great Wall of China, 83
Greenland, 59, 98
Grotte Casteret, 108
Grover's Mill, NJ, 165
gyroscope, 133

H

hair
- beards, 161
- body, 159, 185

Halladay, Roy. 63, 75
hammerhead shark, 38
Hanna's Socks, 190
Hanz and Franz, 17
Harbin International Ice and Snow Festival, 25
Harry Potter, 129
Hawaii, 50, 99. 115, 134
Henson-Conant, Deborah, 125
Hercules (liger), 51
Hex Bug, 139
Hogwarts School of Witchcraft and Wizardry, 129
Hope Diamond, 103
houses
- small, 30-31
- weeHouses, 31

Houston, TX, 29

I

ice
- encasing David Blaine, 133
- in Greenland, 98
- sphinx, 25
- white ice on Enceladus, 115

ice hockey goalies, 66
igloos, 30
India Tower, 149
India, 33, 51, 168
Indian Ocean, 21
Indiana University, 72
Indianapolis 500, 71
Indonesia, 33, 42, 53, 61
Inuit people, 30
insects
- as frogs' food, 61
- cockroaches, 128
- lichen katydid, 48
- mosquito, 157
- termite queen, 40

International Fantasy Hair Competition, 195
International Sand Sculpture Festival, Pera, Portugal, 89
International Space Station, 94, 100
Io, 114
iron in human body, 160
Isner, John, 65

J

Jackson, Michael, 93
Jacobellis, Lindsey, 73
Japan, 65, 84, 94
Jefferson, Thomas, 137
Jupiter, 114-115

K

Kansas City Public Library, 174
Kansas City, MO, 175
Kansas, 126
Kanzi, 55
Keck telescope, 99
Kennedy Space Center, 17
Kennett Square, PA, 172
keratin, 160
Kids vs Global Warming, 191
Komodo dragon, 42-43
Kosen, Sultan, 23
Krubera Cave, 135

L

labyrinth
- Chartres, 179
- definition, 178
- sand, 179

Lake Baikal, 99
Lake Champlain, 169
lamprey, 36
lawnmowers, as race cars, 71
leaves, used as T-shirts, 193, 194
leeches, 37
LEGO®, 131
Legoland, 131
Leshan Giant Buddha, 24
LeTourneau loader, 9
Library of Congress, 175
lichen katydid, 48
liger, 51
Lincoln, Abraham, 27, 67
Lincoln, NE, 128
Lindbergh, Charles, 89
Little Rock, AR, 149
lizard
- frilled, 45
- Komodo dragon, 41-42
- Texas horned, 44
- tuatara, 41

Lockhart, TX, 76
longhorn cattle, as pets, 76
Longleat, 178
Longwood Gardens, 172
Lookout Mountain Caverns, 108
Loorz, Alec, 191
Los Angeles, CA, 29
Louisville Slugger Museum & Factory, 126
lucha libre, 67
lung, re-creation of rat's, 156
Lusitania, 15

M

Macaya breast-spot frog, 61
Madagascar, 33
Mahut, Nicolas, 65
Maine coon cat, 46
Major League Baseball, 63, 75
Manicouagan Crater, 117
Manicouagan Lake, 117
marmoset, 56
Mars, 115
Martin Jetpack, 137, 141
Martin, Glenn, 141
masked lapwing, 159
masks,
- in ice hockey, 66
- in lucha libre, 67

Mason, Steve, 67
Matchstick Marvels Tourist Center, 129
matchsticks, 122, 129
Mauna Kea, 99
Mauna Loa, 115
maze
- definition, 178
- Longleat's hedge, 178
- or labyrinth, 171

McEver, Catherine, 84
mermaids, 51
meteorites
causing craters on Earth, 110-111
causing tsunamis, 97
Methuselah, 40
Mexico, 33, 37, 58, 66, 67, 109
Michigan State University, 66
Michigan, 72
Mickey Mouse, 124
migrations, 58
milkwood leaves, 59
Milky Way, 18, 19, 113
Miller, Ryan, 66
miniature donkeys, 77
mites
dust, 184
eyelash, 185
in human hair, 181
monarch butterfly, 58
monkeys
bonobos, 55
marmosets, 56
Monroe, Marilyn, 128
moon rocks, 103
Moscow, 148
mosquito, 157
motocross, 78
Mount Aconcagua, 104
Mount Elbrus, 105
Mount Everest
climbing, 104
Jordan Romero, 186, 189
Mount Kosciuszko, 105
Mount McKinley (Denali), 104
Mumbai, India, 149
mummies, 193, 197
munchkins, 46
Muniz, Vik, 85
museums, unusual
Burnt Food Museum, 125
Cockroach Hall of Fame, 128
Erika Nelson's traveling museum, 123, 126
Matchstick Marvels Tourist Center, 129
Museum of the Weird, 127, 192
National Museum of Roller Skating, 128
Sickness Bag Virtual Museum, 124
The World's Largest Collection of the World's Smallest Versions of the World's Largest Things, 126
Mushroom Rock State Park, 106
Myers, Andrew, 86, 93
Myhrvold, Nathan, 157

N

nacho hat, 81
nano-bristles, 183
nanomaterials, 182
nanometer, 180, 182
nano-orbs, 183
NASA, 17, 101, 103, 108, 136, 151
NASCAR, 64
National Baseball Hall of Fame, 191
National Museum of Roller Skating, 128
National Stadium in Beijing, 149
NBA, 22
NCAA Men's Basketball Championship, 72
Nelson, Erika, 123, 126
Nepal, 168
neurons, 154, 161
New Hampshire
state quarter, 107
White Mountains, 107
New York City, 29, 100, 132, 133, 144
New York Mets, 73
Niagara River, 132
nictitating membrane, 159
Norfolk, VA, 14
North America, 20, 104, 168, 172
North American plates, 96-97
North Carolina, 72
Notre Dame Cathedral, 132

O

O'Meara, Donna, 130, 134
O'Neal, Shaquille, 22-23
Oasis of the Seas, 15
Obama, Barack, 27, 92
obstacles
in parkour, 63, 68
in snocross, 78
Oh, Sadaharu, 65
Ohio state flag, 67
Ohlendorf, Ross, 76
Old Man of the Mountain, 107
Olympus Mons, 115
Oprah Winfrey Show, 131
owl butterfly, 44
owl, 44

P

Pacific Ocean, 21, 96, 167
Pacific plates, 96
Paris, 132
parkour, 63, 68
patents
the first U.S. patent, 146
Thomas Jefferson, 137
unusual, 146-147
Pearl of Lao Tzu, 103
pearl, 103
Pearson, David, 64
pennies, flattened, 124
Peru, 33
Petit, Philippe, 132
Petra, Jordan, 106
Petty, Richard, 64
Philadelphia Eagles, 77
Philadelphia Phillies, 63, 75
Philadelphia, PA, 100
Phoenix, AZ, 29
Piltdown Man, 161, 164
Piltdown, England, 161, 164
pink handfish, 35
Pittsburgh Pirates, 76
plankton, 58
Plano, TX, 128
Plant City, FL, 191
plants
species in Lake Baikal, 99
why they are stinky, 53
Plastination, 154-155
Polynesia, 167
portraits, 85, 86, 92-93
Predator X, 12
Presley, Elvis, 128
primatologist, 55
pro wrestlers, 66, 67
psittacosaur, 12

Q

Qin Shihuangdi, 90
QTvan, 31
Quay House, 30
Quebec, province of, 117, 169

R

rafflesia, 52
raptorex, 13
red crab, 59

reptiles
frilled lizard, 45
Komodo dragon, 41-42
Texas horned lizard, 44
largest, 43
tuatara, 41
rice weevil, 185
Rio de Janeiro, 88, 148
Rittinger, Dave, 193, 194
Robert Redford Building, 149
Robonaut 2 (R2), 136, 151
robots
EMIEW2, 150
English-teaching, 150
Robonaut 2 (R2), 136, 151
Rochester Institute of Technology, 149
Rochester, NY, 149
roller skates, 128
Romero, Jordan, 186, 189
Rubik's Cube for sightless people, 139
Russia, 58, 105, 148

S

salmon, hybrid, 156
saltwater crocodile, 43
San Francisco, CA, 170
San Jose, CA, 149
sand castles, 88-89
Sand Sculpture Festival, Kagoshima, Japan, 89
sand sculpture
largest, 89
make your own, 89
Santa Monica, CA, 149
Santiago, Chile, 171, 172
Saturn, 111, 115
Science Fiction Museum and Hall of Fame, 174
scorpion fish, 49
seahorses, 56
Seattle, WA, 174
self-portrait, 86, 93
sepia, 48
Seven Summits, 104-105
ships, 14-15
Siberia, 99
Sickness Bag Virtual Museum, 124
Silberberg, Steven, 124
Simmons, Erika Iris, 93
Sims, Ernie, 77
Singapore, 176, 188
skin, human, 160
skunk cabbage, 52
Smithsonian Institution, 103
snocross, 78
snowboarding, 73
snowmobiling
extreme, 62, 78, 79
freestyle, 79
Solar City Tower, 148
Solar Dynamics Observatory (SDO), 118
solar system, 114-115
Sopot, Poland, 175
South Africa, 102
South America, 20, 37, 49, 56, 104, 196
South Pacific Ocean, 35
space
shuttle, 117, 122, 124
trash, 120-121
space shuttle
airsickness bags in, 124
Challenger, 122
Columbia, 117
on flattened pennies, 124
species
in Lake Baikal, 99
new, 34-35
on Earth, 34
percentage in 11 countries, 33
sphinx
cat breed, 47
ice, 25
in ancient Egypt, 25, 51
sports
bloopers and blunders, 72-75
NBA, 22
NCAA, 72
record breakers, 64-65
strange, 68-69
Spy Net Video Watch, 138
stacking, 69
star-nosed mole, 38
Steadfast Foundation. 66
Stonehenge, 126
Stromboli volcano, 130
Summer Olympic Games (2008), 149
Summer Olympic Games (2016), 148
sun
flare, 119
photosphere, 119
prominence, 119
size comparison to Earth, 110, 119
spicules, 119
supernova galaxy, 188

T

T. rex, 12-13
Tarn River, 177
Tenney, MN, 8, 29
teratorn, 168
termite queen, 40
terra cotta army, 82, 87, 90-91
Texas horned lizard, 44
Texas, 127
Thailand, 20
The Wizard of Oz, 46
Thomas, Hank Willis, 92
Tibet, 168
tick, 36
Titanic, 16
toes
human and animal, 153
purpose of, 158
Tokyo Tower, 29
Tokyo, 28-29, 94, 100
Top 5
biggest ancient animals, 13
green buildings in the world, 149
longest land-mammal migrations, 59
most populous U.S. cities, 29
Tour de France, 143
Tower of London, 102
tsunami
definition, 96
how it forms, 97
in Japan, 2011, 96-97
tuatara, 41
Turin, Italy, 73
Turk, The (chess-playing machine), 165
Turkey, 46, 107
Turner, Hannah, 190
Twelve Mile 500 Riding Lawnmower Race, 71
Twelve Mile, IN, 71
Twenty Thousand Leagues Under the Sea, 11
Twin Towers, NYC, 132

U

U.S. Air Force, 101
U.S. Capitol, 129
U.S. Patent and Trademark Office, 137, 146-147
U.S. Presidents
Barack Obama's portrait, 92
on souvenir plates, 123

UCLA, 72
University of Kentucky, 72
University of North Carolina, 72
USS *Enterprise*, 14
USS *Iowa*, 129
Utah, 95

V

vampire bat, 37
vampire flying frog, 34
Van Aelst, Kevin, 84
vegetable bowls, 81
Vermont, 169
vertical gardens
 advantages, 172-173
 hotel in Santiago, Chile, 171, 172
 Longwood Gardens, 172
 Patrick Blanc, 173
Vietnam, 34
Vincent Van Gogh's *Starry Night*, 84
Vinson Massif, 105
Virginia opposum, 45
volcanoes
 Kilauea, 134
 on Io, 114
 on Mars, 115
 shield, 115
 Stromboli, 130
volcanologist, 130, 134
Vomit Comet, 124
von Hagens, Gunther, 154
Vredefort crater, 115

W

War of the Worlds
 broadcast, 163, 165
 monument, 165
Washington, D.C., 103, 175
water bear, 197
waterfalls, 108
Watson, Jessica, 187
Webber, Chris, 72
Wem, Lim Ding, 188
western scrub jay, 54
whale
 bowhead, 40
 false killer, 50
 gray, 58
White House
 details, 26-27
 miniature version, 26-27
white-eared kob, 59
Whitley, John, 123
wholphins, 50
wildebeest, 59
William J. Clinton Presidential Library, 149
Wilson, Mookie, 73
Wimbledon Championships, 65
Winter Olympics (2006), 73
Winter X Games (2011), 78
Wisconsin, 26
wisdom teeth, 159
wolf, 59
Wolfe Creek Crater, 110
woodboring beetle, 181
World Bog Snorkeling Championship, 71
World Chocolate Dream Park, 82
World War I, 15
World's Largest Collection of the World's Smallest Versions of the World's Largest Things, 126
Wright Brothers' plane, 144

X-Y-Z

Xian, China, 90
Yellowstone National Park, 115
yeti crab, 35
Yomiuri Giants, 65
zebroid, 50
zonkey, 50
zony, 50
zorse, 50
Zweifel, John, 26-27

From TIME FOR KIDS

Mini T.rex 13
Little Letters 25
The Incredible Shrinking White House . . . 26-27
Night Stalkers 42
A Great Ape 55
Top 5 Longest Land-Mammal Migrations 59
Killer Waves/How a Tsunami Forms 96-97
Space Junk 121
Craving Caves 135
Great Inventions 140-141
Top 5 Green Buildings in the World 149
Kids Conquer the World 188-189
Kids Make a Big Difference 190-191

Credits

Back cover: NASA (Io); Geanina Bechea/shutterstock (cassowary); Belaya Medvedica/shutterstock.com (sand castle); jigkofoto/shutterstock (bug)

2: jigkofoto/shutterstock (bug); Yadong Yin, Ph. D., Department of Chemistry, University of California, Riverside, CA (watermelon nanopicture); Anyka/shutterstock (butterfly); EcoPrint/shutterstock (owl)

3: Joel Sartore/Getty Images (bat); NASA (bubble); G Navdeep Raj/shutterstock (cuttlefish); Ronald C. Modra/Sports Imagery/Getty Images (Halliday)

4: Andrew Myers/Baldemar Fierro of Laguna Beach, CA (Myers); Nationalparks/Creative Commons (Mushroom Rock State Park); National Museum of Roller Skating, Lincoln, NE, www.rolleskatingmuseum.com (skate); NASA (Enceladus); US Patent and Trademark Office (patent)

5: New York State Historical Association Library, Cooperstown, NY (Cardiff Giant); David Smith/The Canadian Press/AP (kid); Pete Oxford/Minden Pictures (frog); Dmitriy Shironosov/shutterstock (toes)

6-7: jigkofoto/shutterstock (bug)

8-9: Amy Walters/shutterstock (hand with magnifying glass); jigkofoto/shutterstock (bug); Brain Rodeo (Tenney); Tood Bigelow–Aurora for TFK (White House miniature); Qingdao Qizhou Rubber Co., Ltd. (loader)

10-11: Barry Durrant/Getty Images (giant squid); Brian J. Skerry/Getty Images (eye); Robert F. Sisson/National Geographic/Getty Images (mouth); Brian J. Skerry/Getty Images (tentacles); public domain (Verne)

12-13: REUTERS/Atlantic Productions/Zoo/Handout (Predator X); Andrey Armyagor (snorkeling kid); Nobu Tamura, www.palaeocritti.com (psittacosaur); Mike Hettwer (raptorex); Creative Commons (beelzebufo)

14-15: Douglas M. Pearlman/U.S. Navy/Getty Images (USS *Enterprise*); Henrik Kettunen/Bloomberg via Getty Images (*Allure of the Seas*); MPI/Getty Images (*Lusitania*)

16-17: Martin Röll/Creative Commons (Bagger 288); NASA (Hanz & Franz)

18-19: David Erck, www.ExtremeBubbles.com (bubble); NASA (space bubble); Julian Rovagnati/shutterstock (kid with chewing gum)

20-21: jigkofoto/shutterstock (bug); Christian Musat/shutterstock (capybara); Norbert Wu/Minden Pictures (giant clam)

22-23: Greg Nelson/Sports Illustrated (hand); Leon Neal/AFP/Getty Images (kid with Kosen's hand); Mustafa Ozer/AFP/Getty Images (Kosen); Greg Nelson/Sports Illustrated (O'Neal)

24-25: Liu Jin/AFP/Getty Images (Buddha); Solent News (pencils); Lukas Hlavac/shutterstock.com (Harbin)

26-27: Todd Bigelow–Aurora for TFK

28-29: nujimomo/shutterstock (Tokyo); Chris 73/Creative Commons (Tokyo subway); Brain Rodeo (Tenney)

30-31: Creative Commons (house in Great Britain, igloo); Courtesy of Alchemy (weeHouses); Yannick Read, www.eta.co.uk (QTvan)

32-33: Creatista/shutterstock (kid); Paul Marcus/shutterstock (corpse flower); Patrick Rolands/shutterstock (komodo dragon)

34-35: Jodi J. L. Rowley (all frog photos); AP Photo/Ifremer, A. Fifis (hairy crab); David Hall/Getty Images (handfish)

36-37: Norbert Wu/Getty Images (lamprey); David Pedre/Getty Images (lamprey's mouth); Hansel Mieth/Time Life Pictures/Getty Images (tick comparison); Shilo Watts/Getty Images (tick on skin); Joel Sartore/Getty Images (bat); Natalia Kolesnikova/AFP/Getty Images (leeches)

38-39: Dembinsky Photo Ass./FLPA/Minden Pictures (mole); Ian Scott/shutterstock (shark); Geanina Bechea/shutterstock (cassowary); Worakit Sirijinda/shutterstock (cassowary, bottom left)

40-41: Flip Nicklin/Minden Pictures (whale); Derek Gordon/shutterstock (tree); China Photos/Getty Images (termite queen); Joel Sartore/National Geographic/Getty Images (sturgeon); Cameramannz/shutterstock (tuatara)

42-43: Dean Bertonceli/shutterstock (komodo dragon); Map by TFK; Macduff Everton/Corbis (baby and mother); David Lee/shutterstock (crocodile)

44-45: Zylorian/Creative Commons (Texas horned lizard); Anyka/shutterstock (butterfly); EcoPrint/shutterstock (owl); public domain (opposum); Natphotos/Getty Images (frilled lizard)

46-47: All photos by Creative Commons

48-49: G Navdeep Raj/shutterstock (cuttlefish); Michael & Patricia Fogden/Minden Pictures (katydid); Michael & Patricia Fogden/Minden Pictures (viper); Olga Khoroshunova/shutterstock (scorpion fish)

50-51: Creative Commons (zonkey); Todd Pusser/npl/Minden Pictures (wholphin); www.LigerLiger.com (liger); Nestor Noci/shutterstock (sphinx); Vasily Mulyukin/shutterstock (centaur)

52-53: Ingo Arndt/Minden Pictures (rafflesia buds); kkaplin/shutterstock (rafflesia); Paula Cobleigh/shutterstock (skunk cabbage); Paul Marcus/shutterstock (corpse flower)

54-55: Dim Stern/shutterstock.com (dolphins); Thomas W. Woodruff/shutterstock (jay); Sophie Tachna (dog); Finlay McKay for TIME (ape)

56-57: Manamana/shutterstock (monkeys); Martina Ebel/shutterstock (seahorses); Fred Olivier/npl/Minden Pictures (emperor penguins, top); Gentoo Multimedia Ltd./shutterstock (emperor penguins, bottom)

58-59: jocrebbin/shutterstock (gray whale); Christian Musat/shutterstock (butterfly); Arto Hakola/shuttestock (tern); Travel Ink/Getty Images (crabs); Top 5, top to bottom: Tom Walker/Getty Images; Juniors Bildarchiv/Photolibrary; John E. Marriott/Photolibrary; P. Jaccod/Getty Images; Alan Dragesco-Joffe/Photolibrary

60-61: Timothy Laman/National Geographic/Getty Images (flying frog); Paul Zahl/National Geographic/Getty Images (goliath frog); Robin Moore (breast-spot frog); David Bickford/AP (aquatic brown frog)

62-63: Danilo Moura/shutterstock (basketball); Christian Pondella/Getty Images (snowmobile); Brooke Whatnall/shutterstock (parkour)

64-65: Walter G Arce/shutterstock.com (Petty); Ben Stansall/AFP/Getty Images (Mahut); Dave Thompson/AFP/Getty Images (Isner); Diamond Images/Getty Images (Oh, 1971); Kazuhiro Nogi/AFP/Getty Images (Oh)

66-67: Len Redkoles/NHLI via Getty Images (Miller, front); Al Tielemans/Sports Illustrated (Miller, back); Graig Abel/NHLI via Getty Images (Mason, left); Jamie Sabau/NHLI via Getty Images (Mason, right); Creative Commons (lucha libre masks)

68-69: Brooke Whatnall (parkour); Justin Steele for TIME (stacking); Courtesy of John S. Kennedy, United States Bycicle Polo Association (bike polo)

70-71: Courtesy of New York Road Runners (run-up); Jorg Hackemann/shutterstock.com (Empire State building); Richard Heathcote/Getty Images (bog snorkeling); Mark Bever (lawnmower race)

72-73: David E. Klutho/Sports Illustrated (Webber); Stan Grossfeld/The Boston Globe via Getty Images (Buckner); Bob Martin/Sports Illustrated (Jacobellis)

74-75: Elsa/Getty Images (Castillo); Creative Commons (Chicago Cubs); Bill Eisner/Detroit Tigers/Getty Images (Galarraga); Mark Cunningham/MLB Photos via Getty Images (signs); Ronald C. Modra/Sports Imagery/Getty Images (Halladay)

76-77: Darren Carroll/Sports Illustrated (Ohlendorf); Andrew Hancock/Sports Illustrated (Sims); Rich Frishman/Sports Illustrated (Deneen)

78-79: Doug Pensinger/Getty Images (left); Christian Pondella/Getty Images (right)

80-81: Raúl Rodriguez (nacho hat); Andersen Ross/Getty Images (girl); Margaret Dorfman (bowl); Valeria Potapova/shutterstock (chocolate bars)

82-83: All photos by testing/shutterstock.com

84-85: Catherine McEver, stuffyoucanthave.blogspot.com (bread); public domain (Van Gogh); Kevin Van Aelst (apple); John Kobal Foundation/Getty Images (Karloff); © Vik Muniz/Licensed by VAGA, New York, NY (*Frankenstein*, 2004)

86-87: Andrew Myers/Baldemar Fierro of Laguna Beach, CA (Myers); Diem Chau, www.diemchau.com (*Zodiac Crayons*, private collection; *Currency Crayons*, collection of Davis and Louise Riemer); Lukas Hlavac/shutterstock (terra cotta army)

88-89: Antonio Scorza/AFP/Getty Images (Rio); wdeon/shutterstock.com (Japan); BelayaMedvedica/shutterstock.com (Portugal) Creative Commons (China)

90-91: asliuzunoglu/shutterstock (full spread photo); Lukas Hlavac/shutterstock (heads)

92-93: Hank Willis Thomas & Ryan Alexiev/Photo by Amy Cheng (Obama); Andrew Myers/Baldemar Fierro of Laguna Beach, CA (Myers' self-portrait); Erika Iris Simmons (Jackson); Andrew Buckin/shutterstock (cassette)

94-95: Courtesy of the Image Science & Analysis Laboratory, NASA Johnson Space Center (Tokyo); Logan Carter/shutterstock (arch)

96-97: Joe LeMonnier for TFK (maps); Mainichi Newspaper/EPA (tsunami photo); Jim Kopp for TFK (diagrams)

98-99: NASA (Greenland); David Aleksandrowicz/shutterstock (telescope); Ran Z/shutterstock (Dead Sea); BelayaMedvedica (Lake Baikal)

100-101: All photos courtesy of the Image Science & Analysis Laboratory, NASA Johnson Space Center

102-103: John Whitley (Star of Africa); Paul J. Richards/AFP/Getty Images (Hope Diamond); public domain (Pearl of Lao Tzu)

104-105: Daniel Prudek/shutterstock (Everest); Suwandichandra Photography/shutterstock (Denali); George F. Mobley/National Geographic/Getty Images (Aconcagua); Thomas Senf/Euro-Newsroom via Getty Images (Elbrus); Graeme Shannon/shutterstock (Kilimanjaro); SimplySW (Kosciuszko); NASA (Vinson Massif)

106-107: meunierd/shutterstock (Petra); Nationalparks/Creative Commons (Mushroom Rock State Park); public domain (Old Man of the Mountain and coin) steba/shutterstock (Goreme Valley)

108-109: Jtesla16/Creative Commons (Ruby Falls); Carsten Peter/ Speleoresearch & Films/National Geographic/Getty Images (caves)

110-111: David Petit/shutterstock (crater); NASA (Enceladus and sun)

112-113: All photos by NASA/JPL-Caltech

114-115: All photos courtesy of NASA

116-117: David Petit/shutterstock (Wolf Creek Crater); STS-9 Crew, NASA (Manicouagan Crater); NASA (Vrededfort Crater)

118-119: All photos courtesy of NASA

120-121: All photos courtesy of NASA

122-123: Patrick Acton, www.matchstickmarvels.com (left); Erika Nelson (top); John Whitley (bottom)

124-125: Ronald Dupont Jr. (pennies); www.airsicknessbags.com (bags); The Bone Room, www.boneroom.com (displays); Deborah Henson-Conant, curator, www.BurntFoodMuseum.com (burnt food)

126-127: Erika Nelson (Carhenge and Louisville Slugger); Nicole Tan/shutterstock (Stonehenge); Courtesy of Museum of the Weird, Steve Busti (Bigfoot)

128-129: National Museum of Roller Skating, Lincoln, NE, www.rolleskatingmuseum.com (skates); Cockroach Hall of Fame, Plano, TX, www.pestshop.com/cockroaches.html (Monroe); Patrick Acton, www.matchstickmarvels.com (U.S. Capitol and Hogwarts School of Witchcraft and Wizardry)

130-131: © Steve and Donna O'Meara (O'Meara); Spencer Platt/ Newsmakers/Getty Images (Blaine); Mariann Asanuma, www.modelbuildingsecrets.com (Asanuma)

132-133: Keystone-France/Gamma-Keystone via Getty Images (Petit); Spencer Platt/Newsmakers/Getty Images (Blaine, top); Timothy A. Clary/ AFP/Getty Images

134-135: © Steve and Donna O'Meara (O'Meara); James Tabor (supercave)

136-137: NASA (robot); Derek Henderson for TIME (jetpack); U.S. Patent and Trademark Office (dog ear protector)

138-139: www.spynethq.com (Spy Net); Innovation First International, www.innovationfirst.com (hex bugs); Rubik's® use of image by kind permission of Seven Towns Limited (Rubik's Cube)

140-141: Raytheon (parachute); Minesto (kite); Kimball Hall/Hydronalix (Emily); Wenn.com/Newscom (AirPod car); Derek Henderson for TIME (jetpack)

142-143: Tony Kyriacou/Rex Features (bendable bike); Xylonbikes (Xylon); VW (VW bik.e); Ferderic B/shutterstock.com (Tour de France)

144-145: All airplane photos courtesy of Airbus A380; Rob Wilson/ shutterstock (schoolbus)

146-147: All images from U.S. Patent and Trademark Office except #5, by Felipe Galindo

148-149: Rafael Schmidt, RAFAA design, www.rafaa.ch (solar city tower); Creative Commons (mega mall); Ryan Browne, Cook+Fox Architects/ Creative Commons (Bank of America)

150-151: Nippon News/Zumapress.com (EMIEW2); Koo Sung Soo for TIME (English-teaching robot); NASA (R2)

152-153: © Gunther von Hagens, Institute for Plastination, Heidelberg, Germany, www.bodyworlds.com. All rights reserved (Body Worlds); Jaime Chung for TIME (EyeWriter); A_Sh/shutterstock (orangutan); Dmitriy Shironosov/shutterstock (toes)

154-155: All photos © Gunther von Hagens, Institute for Plastination, Heidelberg, Germany, www.bodyworlds.com. All rights reserved

156-157: Jaime Chung for TIME (lung); Aquabounty Technologies (salmon); Ryan Matthew Smith/Intellectual Ventures (mosquito); Bartholomew Cooke for TIME (robotic legs)

158-159: Vinicius Tupinamba/shutterstock (eyes); Poulsons Photography/shutterstock (toes); Creative Commons (masked lapwing); Leonello Calvetti/shutterstock (appendix); Roblan/shutterstock (leg)

160-161: mathagraphics/shuttestock (background)

162-163: Anrie/Creative Commons (Piltdown Man); Jabberocky/Creative Commons (crop circle); Bruce Rolff/shutterstock (UFO & planet)

164-165: New York State Historical Association Library, Cooperstown, NY (Cardiff Giant); public domain (Turk); NY Daily News Archive via Getty Images (War of the Worlds); public domain (monument)

166-167: Hansueli Krapf/Creative Commons (crop circle, top); Jabberocky/Creative Commons (crop circle, bottom); Andrzej Gibasiewicz/shutterstock (Easter Island, top); Vladimir Korostyshevskiy/ shutterstock.com (Easter Island, bottom)

168-169: De Agostini Picture Library/De Agostini/Getty Images (bird); andreisss (Yeti scalp); public domain (Champ)

170-171: Lowe Llaguno/shutterstock (Golden Gate Bridge); José Luis Stephens for TIME (garden wall); Till F. Teenck/Creative Commons (maze)

172-173: Creative Commons (Longwood Gardens); José Luis Stephens for TIME (garden wall); Dag Sundberg/Getty Images (Blanc)

174-175: All photos by Creative Commons

176-177: Weesen photos/Getty Images (Henderson Waves Bridge); Leonard G./Creative Commons (Rolling Bridge); Eric Cabanis/AFP/ Getty Images (Millau Viaduct)

178-179: Jason Hawkes/Getty Images (maze); Sandra Kilpatrick Jordan (sand labyrinth); EcOasis/shutterstock (Chartres labyrinth)

180-181: Yadong Yin, Ph. D., Department of Chemistry, University of California, Riverside, CA (nanopicture); Jubal Harshaw/shutterstock (mite); Henrik Larsson/shutterstock (beetle)

182-183: Xudong Wang and Jian Shi, Department of Materials Science and Engineering, University of Wisconsin, Madison, WI (flower nanopicture); Boaz Pokroy, Department of Materials Engineering, Technion, Tel Aviv (nano ball); Yadong Yin, Ph. D., Department of Chemistry, University of California, Riverside, CA (watermelon nanopicture)

184-185: Jubal Harshaw/shutterstock (mite); Liew Weng Keong/ shutterstock (rice weevil); Joel Mills/Creative Commons (eyelash mite); Creative Commons (human hair)

186-187: Prakash Mathema/AFP/Getty Images (Romero); Torsten Blackwood/AFP/Getty Images (Watson)

188-189: David Smith/The Canadian Press/AP (Gray); Vivek Prakash/ Reuters (Lim Ding Wen); Prakash Mathema/AFP/Getty Images (Romero); Pichugin Dmitry/shutterstock (Mt Everest)

190-191: Kim Koluch/Considering Lilies Photography (Turner); Andy Holzman/Los Angeles Daily News/Zumapress.com (Cassini); Jordan Raines/Meet the Famous/Newsroom (Baker); Victoria Loorz (Loorz)

192-193: Courtesy of Museum of the Weird, Steve Busti (Cabinet of Curiosities); Dave Rittinger, *Zero Footprint Shirts*, from the *Leaf Series*, 2010, www.daverittinger.com (leaf shirt); Pete Oxford/Minden Pictures (frog); Sabina Louise Pierce/The New York Times (mummy)

194-195: Dave Rittinger, *Zero Footprint Shirts*, from the *Leaf Series*, 2010, www.daverittinger.com (leaf shirt); Jim Cole/AP (hair competition); The Bone Room, www.boneroom.com (chocolate and lollipops)

196-197: Pete Oxford/Minden Pictures (frog); Goldstein Lab, UNC Chapel Hill (water bear); Sabina Louise Pierce/The New York Times (mummy)

208: Elnur/shutterstock (cell phone)

Maps: vector images by shutterstock, modified by R studio T, unless indicated otherwise. All backgrounds by shutterstock, unless indicated otherwise.

R U in the Hunt?

U just got a text message! Check it out. It has clues to finding the names of people, places, and things in this book. Track down each clue and then write the first letter of the answer in the blanks below, on a separate piece of paper, or on your cell phone. Unscramble the 10 letters to spell out a word that describes you. GLE1! :–) (The answer is upside down below.)

INBOX

From: Jonathan

Go 2 p. 169: monster in a lake ROFL

Go 2 p. 131: some XLNT building blocks

Go 2 p. 64: 1st name of man who can XLR8

Go 2 p. 143: Robo keeps swimmers safe

Go 2 p. 182: the scale U use to measure teeny objects. C intro

Go 2 p. 140: 2nd word in headline

Go 2 p. 176: find a bridge that unrolls in this country

Go 2 p. 50: cross this and horse and U get a mule

Go 2 p. 55: Kanzi is this kind of ape

Go 2 p. 13: 1st name of biggest penguin EVA

REPLY **Options**

___ ___ ___ ___ ___ ___ ___ ___ ___ ___

Answer: CHAMP, LEGOS, RICHARD, EMILY, NANOMETER, INVENTION, ENGLAND, DONKEY, BONOBO, INKAYAKU. The unscrambled letters spell out INCREDIBLE.